To my way of thinking, it is time! For the covenant people, it is time!

History of the Saints

IN THE
Midst
OF THEE

VOLUME I

REVISED 3RD EDITION

GLENN RAWSON AND DENNIS LYMAN

ISBN 978-1-7355962-1-1
Printed In the United States of America.

Acknowledgments

This note is to say thank you to all those who have helped bring these stories to a large and receptive audience. Many thanks go to my family and friends for letting me tell their stories. Carl Watkins deserves much thanks. These stories were his brainchild. Brian and Rachel Hansen will always be among my dearest friends. It was they who first compiled this volume.

This revised second edition comes in response to a continued demand for the stories. Long after we thought this book and its companion volume had "run their course," they are still being asked for. We offer this new edition in the hope that it may bring peace, inspiration, and hope in difficult times.

CONTENTS

HAPPINESS 1

WATER-SKIING 4

WATCH THE LAMB 6

ELIJAH 8

CLOSE ENOUGH TO TOUCH 10

DRUSILLA HENDRICKS 12

THE PALSIED MAN AND HIS FRIENDS 14

WHEN YOU BELIEVE 16

NICKNAMES 19

ALLELOPATHY 21

TEACHING, A SACRED TRUST 22

KIDNEY STONES 24

RACHEL AND ADRIAN 27

PRAYER 30

TRUST THE PILOT 33

TOM 35

THOU ART THE CHRIST 37

THE VISION OF ENOCH 39

MITCHIE 41

"HE CARES" 43

LIFE ISN'T FAIR 45

WHITEWASHED 46

DADDY 48

THE WEEPING WOMAN 49

ORANGE JUICE 50

THE MARATHON 52

STATE TROOPER 54

THE CHRISTMAS STORY 56

TO THE TEACHERS 58

THE LAMB OF GOD 61

"ARE YOU JOHN PETER MALMBERG?" 63

THE BATTLE HAS BEGUN 65

KATIE'S PRAYER 67

THE ROCK OF OFFENSE 69

MARYANN'S RACE 71

MY MIND IS MINE 73

EASTER AND RACHEL 75

BREAKING A HORSE 77

REFLECTIONS ON A SKI TRIP 79

ISAIAH 53 81

"COME BACK, ELLA, COME BACK"—
ELLA JENSEN AND
PRESIDENT LORENZO SNOW 83

FAITH TO WALK ON WATER 86

THE SOIL 88

HIS BLOOD 90

THE CLEANSING 92

TOOTH FAIRY 94

SOUTH TETON 96

THE EASTER STORY 98

PRODIGAL SON 101

BUT IF NOT 102

GIDEON 104

"DADDY, HELP!" 106

BAND-AIDS AND SUNSETS 109

COURAGE TO DO RIGHT 111

LOVE ONE ANOTHER 113

SUMMER THUNDER 115

NAAMAN'S MIRACLE 117

JED'S PRAYER 119

MOTHERING UP 121

THE STORMS OF LIFE 123

THE POWER OF HIS NAME 126

I LOVE YOU 128

"Father, Let Us Go On" 130

The Skunk 132

Power 134

That One Year 135

Shaina's Rock 137

Angie's Solo 139

Moses and the Serpent 141

Chopsticks and Jell-O 143

Smile at the Stoplight 145

Telephone Wire 147

All Creatures of the Spring 149

The Switch 151

"George, Do You Know Me?" 153

Lord, I Believe 156

The Lunar Eclipse 158

The Gentile Woman 160

THE WIDOW'S MITE 162

DAWNI'S DISAPPOINTMENT 164

THE STORY OF EASTER 166

TENDERIZING 168

SARAH AND THE ANGELS 170

ROAD RAGE 172

CLIFFORD IN SPANISH 174

"GO TO THE PLACE OF GATHERING" 176

MAX AND JOYCE 178

BAD THINGS TO GOOD PEOPLE 180

LIVING ON THE EDGE 182

EMMELINE 184

HANNAH HENDEE 186

COURTNEY'S SECOND CHANCE 188

ENOS 190

THE FLAGPOLE 192

MAMA'S BOYS 194

RUTH 196

"GOD HELPS THOSE WHO HELP THEMSELVES" . . . 198

TURN TO PRAY 202

PEACE 204

CHANGE 205

PEACE ON EARTH 207

THE LOCKSMITH 209

FORWARD MOMENTUM 211

GETHSEMANE 213

"HE DID STRENGTHEN THEM" 215

INDEX 217

HAPPINESS

Sometimes I think we live in a grumpy world!—and it is so unnecessary. There is no need for any person to be lastingly miserable.

When the Savior said, "be of good cheer," it was a commandment, not a suggestion (John 16:33).

Once, while serving as a missionary on a very cold Midwest winter morning, my companion and I went out to meet people. In an effort to ward off the cold and discouragement, we began telling jokes to one another. As we approached a stranger's door, my companion told me a joke, and I didn't get it—it went right over my head.

I continued, however, pondering the punch line. Then, just as the door began to open, I got it! And it was hilarious! I started laughing so hard I could hardly talk, as did my companion.

When the lady of the house opened the door, she saw two young men on her doorstep, laughing uproariously! I tried to stifle my mirth long enough to state our purpose for being there. But I'm afraid it came out more as a series of garbled snorts and chokings. I don't think to this day she knew what I said, but the wonderful thing of it all, and the reason I tell you this story, is that she began laughing also. Soon we were all having a good laugh. She was still chuckling as she closed the door and sent us on our way, as we were.

My friends, life is wonderful, and there is so much to enjoy and laugh at—and it's not wrong. And if we come to the Savior, who was the most cheerful of all men who ever lived, He will teach us how to find the happiness and the joy that was the purpose of our creation in the first place.

ROBB AND CALEB

S ometimes the most powerful of sermons are not what we say; they're what we do.

One day I was sitting in my church services listening to a young man who had just returned from two years in Detroit, Michigan. The first thing that impressed me was how much Robb had grown while he was gone. He'd always been a big young man, a rodeo cowboy, well over six feet tall with a powerful build. But now, there was a spiritual bigness about Robb. You couldn't see it, but you could feel it.

Robb spoke on the theme of "letting your light shine before men," and he told of touching experiences with young children and elderly ladies. It was a sight to see. More than once this big, tenderhearted cowboy was melted to tears as he spoke of people he had loved and reached out to in Michigan. His sermon was well spoken.

When the meeting was over, the congregation began to sing the closing hymn. A young father, Marcus, stood up to direct the music. His little boy, Caleb, followed him up to the stand. As the song got underway and Dad's arm got into motion, Caleb suddenly decided it was time for exploration and adventure. He began moving farther and farther away from his dad, running back and forth and in and out around the choir seats, having the time of his life, and all this to the entertainment of the entire congregation.

From where I was sitting, it was obvious that Dad was uncomfortable. At first, he just kept looking over his shoulder to see what Caleb was doing. But as Caleb got farther out, Dad got more and more nervous. Then Dad stopped singing. Finally, Dad stopped leading altogether and turned around and motioned for Caleb to come back. Caleb only grinned broadly and ran in the opposite direction. Now, what was Dad going to do? Junior was making a scene and disrupting the whole meeting. Should he skip the music, take off, and chase the boy down, making it worse, or should he let Caleb go and pray that Caleb doesn't make it any worse? It was a dilemma. What's Dad going to do?

Suddenly and without any warning, my big cowboy friend stood up and walked back into the choir seats where Caleb was playing. Caleb saw him coming, and he started to run, thinking it would be a chase. But Robb simply sat down and with a big grin on his face and motioned for Caleb to come to him. Cautiously at first, Caleb sidled over to Robb, and Robb scooped him up on his lap and began talking to him. To my surprise, Caleb nestled inside those big arms like he had known Robb all his life, and there he stayed for the rest of the meeting.

It's hard to describe how that affected me. I guess being a dad, I have a soft spot for that. But in two quiet minutes with a tiny child, Robb taught me more about letting your light so shine before men than in the entire twenty minutes of his talk. I want to be more like that.

I pray the Lord to bless me that my actions will always cash the checks that my words so freely write.

From an experience in the Blackfoot 7th Ward sacrament meeting involving Marcus and Caleb Adams and Robb Dansie.

WATER-SKIING

Recently I had an experience that powerfully reinforced the principle that one cannot truly appreciate the joy of conquering something unless he has painfully failed a few times.

I was invited by some friends to go water-skiing. Now, I have never water-skied in my life, and what's more, I can't even swim. When I get in water over my head, my panic button goes bonkers; I float like a rock. So, I don't know whether it was male ego or a fit of foolishness, but I agreed to go.

When it came my turn, I was given some brief instructions. Bobbing like a cork, I finally managed to strap those ungainly boards on my feet that for some reason were always trying to get above my head. When I was finally set, I signaled for Wade to hit it. Oh—oh, and he did! I think I drank half the lake before I finally let go of that silly rope.

I rounded up the skis to try again, and this time I made it up on the skis, but I couldn't keep a steady pressure on the towrope. Wade accelerated to take up the slack when suddenly my ski tips caught. The next thing I knew, I was flying through the air Superman style hanging onto that rope. When I finally hit the water at thirty miles an hour, I had no idea something as soft as water could hurt so much!

I was ready to say, "That's it! That's enough! I'm too old for this much fun." But, when I could finally breathe again, my dad's words from childhood came to me: "When you get bucked off, boy, you get back on!"

It was with some trepidation that I put those boards back on my feet. As I sat there poised to hit it again, I found myself saying, "Heavenly Father, I have to do this. Please help me!"

Well, Wade gunned the boat, and I popped right up, and to my joy, this time I stayed up. And you know, it was fun! I made a couple of passes around the lake until I was comfortable, and then once more I crashed rather ingloriously when I tried crossing the wake. But I had gotten up, and little by little as the day went on, my skill and my confidence increased until the last time I skied I was glad to finally crash. I had been up so long and skied so many times around the lake, I was too tired to hang on anymore.

Here's the point: Whether it's water-skiing or overcoming the natural man, the principle is the same. We learn to rise above this murky mortal lake of wickedness we live in by painfully crashing into it a few times. Those crashes hurt, but they are necessary, and they are expected. How else can we learn? But I promise you, if we will grit our teeth, pray hard, and try again, we will rise above it until someday we will by the grace of God become skilled enough to stay above it.

Oh, and one more thing: I assure you, no matter how humiliating and embarrassing the wreck, God always comes back for you.

WATCH THE LAMB

The Apostle John made a statement in the book of Revelation: "Worthy is the lamb that was slain" (Revelation 5:12).

Nearly two thousand years ago, the Jews of Jesus's day commemorated the Passover, that sacred event from their history when the angel of death passed over them while all the firstborn among the Egyptians died.

On Thursday, sometime in the late afternoon, Peter and John, at the Savior's command, took a lamb and, under the direction of the priests in the temple, killed it and spilled its blood. They then prepared the Passover for Jesus and the rest of the Twelve. That evening He and they came to partake of the last officially authorized paschal lamb.

For four thousand years, God's people had been sacrificing lambs and shedding their blood as an offering for sin. Even now, thousands of lambs would be killed over two days' time.

For years, the thought of such a thing—especially as part of my religious devotions—seemed distasteful and disgusting. Why would God have commanded such a thing of them?

Well, I don't know all the reasons. But as I studied it and thought about it, I learned some interesting things. The lamb was a symbol to point them to the time when their Redeemer would come and be the final offering. For example, consider some of the following:

Each of the lambs selected was male, unblemished, and perfect, just as Jesus would be.

Each was innocent and undeserving of his fate, just as Jesus would be.

Each was meekly submissive, just as Jesus would be.

Each was brought by the head of the household to be sacrificed on behalf of the family, just as Jesus would be.

Each had his blood forcefully shed and thus his life taken, just as Jesus's life would be taken.

Each was sacrificed in the holy place, just as Jesus would be in the holy city.

Each Passover lamb was sacrificed under the authority of Israel's priests, just as Jesus would be.

Each was sacrificed without a bone broken, just as Jesus would be.

Each lamb was of the first year, cut off in the bloom of life, just as Jesus would be.

And each had another's sins placed upon it and vicariously died for them, just as Jesus would.

After the shedding of great drops of atoning blood in Gethsemane, Jesus was led away like a lamb to Golgotha, where on Friday morning, He was lifted up and sacrificed. For some six hours, He hung in indescribable agony. Then sometime around three o'clock in the afternoon, perhaps even while the paschal lambs were dying in the temple, Jesus died, the ultimate offering for the sins of the world. And in His offering, I have part. Because of it, I am encircled in the arms of mercy. No more were the lambs to die. It was not necessary. The horrible price was paid. Man was free!

For many years I was tempted to rail and accuse those who missed the significance of the lambs and their blood when it was fulfilled, until it occurred to me that unless and until I understand the significance of the bread and the wine, I had better be quiet. May the Lord bless us to more fully watch the lamb and understand the offering that has been made for us.

ELIJAH

Elijah of the Old Testament was considered the prophet of the prophets. And yet during his ministry, an event occurred from which I draw great strength in tough times.

Elijah labored with his whole soul to bring the nation of Israel unto Jehovah, even calling down incredible displays of divine power to persuade the people. But still he was rejected and hated by the very people he came to save.

Running for his life, Elijah fled into the wilderness, where he made a most interesting request of the Lord.

He said, "It is enough; now, O Lord, take away my life; for I am not better than my fathers" (1 Kings 19:4).

Now, I don't mean to make light of it, but that sounds like a very burdened and discouraged prophet.

If someone as great as that can be overwhelmed and want to give up, what about you and me?

The story doesn't end there, though. In the spirit of fasting and prayer, Elijah went deeper into the wilderness, all the way to Sinai, where the word of the Lord came to him and asked, "[Elijah,] What doest thou here . . . ?" (1 Kings 19:9).

And in response, Elijah poured out his soul to God.

Notably, when Elijah finished, God did not pity him or commiserate. What good would it do? Instead, He brought Elijah out upon the mount, and there began an awesome display of the powers of nature—wind and earthquake and fire. But the record says God was not in them, meaning—at least, as I see it—that after it was over, Elijah was impressed but still discouraged (see 1 Kings 19:11–12).

Then there came a "still small voice" from God, the voice of His Spirit, and Elijah was healed. It spoke peace to his wounded, burdened heart. And the result: Elijah got up and went back to work with renewed zeal (see 1 Kings 19:12–14).

Is it hard sometimes to swim in the deep waters of mortality? Is there a tendency at times to want to give up? And I ask, is the Lord angry with us on those days when we just can't go on? When we just can't do it anymore? No! Not the Lord I know, not when we're trying to be good. And the still, small voice that spoke peace to Elijah is as much ours to claim as it was his—if in our prayers we reach deeper than the trite phrases and get to where the heart really is.

CLOSE ENOUGH TO TOUCH

You know, there are some problems that arise in our lives that are just beyond the scope of our ability to solve. And I think a wise and loving Heavenly Father has made sure of that. Why? Well, if we could solve every problem, answer every question, and cope with every crisis ourselves, what need would we have of Him? My friends, there is a much better world than this one waiting for those who in their extremity reach out for His power.

Thronged by a crowd, Jesus follows the anxious Jairus on an errand to heal his dying daughter. Within that crowd is a woman afflicted with an incurable disease. In seeking a cure, she has spent all her fortune, yet even now she is not healed, but rather more sickly than ever.

Somehow, she learns of the great healer and determines to go to Him, but because of the nature of her illness, she is ashamed to ask for His help.

As Jesus passes in the crowd with Jairus, she says to herself, "If I may but touch [the hem of] his garment, I shall be whole" (Matthew 9:21).

She pushes her way through the crowd, and from behind, she touches the Master's robe. Immediately there is a tangible surge of power that flows throughout the woman's body. She is fully healed from that very moment!

Filled with emotion and gratitude, she drops back into the crowd, out of sight. However, Jesus stops, turns around, and scans the crowd.

"Who touched me?" He asks (Luke 8:45).

In effect, Peter says to Him, "There are all these people pushing and shoving, and you ask 'Who touched me?'"

Jesus makes it clear, though, that this touch was different from any other. "I perceive," He says, "that virtue is gone out of me" (Luke 8:46).

The woman, knowing that she was discovered, comes forward, falls at His feet, and confesses what she has done. With kindness and tenderness, the Master commends her for her faith.

"Daughter," He says, "thy faith hath made thee whole; go in peace" (Luke 8:48).

This woman felt unworthy of Him, yet she compelled herself forward, driven by an overwhelming sense that she simply had nowhere else to go. That is how we exercise faith. We push ourselves toward Him, especially when we don't feel like it. And now as then, there will come power into our lives, the power to heal, the power to change, but only if we will come close enough to touch.

Adapted from Matthew 9:20–22, Mark 5:25–34, and Luke 8:43–48.

DRUSILLA HENDRICKS

We admire our pioneer ancestors for their courage and their sacrifice, and well we should. We read about what they did, and we stand back in awe, wondering if we could do the same in our day. In that spirit, may I share the "touching" story of Drusilla Hendricks?

In 1839, Drusilla was living the happiest days of her life, with a new home, a new faith, and a loving family. Then one night, her world was changed. Her husband, James, was shot in the neck by a mob, leaving him paralyzed from the neck down. The mob then drove her from her home and ransacked it. The family returned to their home only to then be ordered to leave the state immediately.

Drusilla sold the family land for enough money to buy oxen to pull a small wagon, and she then set out for Illinois in the cold, winter weather of early March. When she finally settled, friends built a log cabin for her, which she then chinked and plastered herself.

After that, to make ends meet, Drusilla, with a family of five children under the age of eleven, began raising a large garden, taking in boarders, and selling homemade gingerbread and mittens. Drusilla worked hard; she did all that she could to support herself.

But again, their peace was only temporary. Mobs again descended upon her people, and in the winter of 1846, Drusilla again loaded up her family, crossed the Mississippi River, and turned her face to the west.

They had not gone far, however, when word came that volunteers were needed to join the United States Army in a war with Mexico. By now Drusilla's oldest son, William, was eighteen, and William wanted to join the army. For seven years, this son had been her greatest help. There was no way. How could she give him up? How in the world would she survive a more than thousand-mile journey across the wilderness without him? There was no way.

Then one morning, as Drusilla was preparing to fix breakfast, the familiar voice of the Spirit spoke to her in words such as these:

"Drusilla, do you desire the greatest glory of heaven?"

"Yes, Lord," she answered.

"Then, how can you get it without making sacrifices?"

"Lord, what lack I yet?"

The voice of the Lord came softly, "Let your son go in the battalion."

William joined the army with his mother's urging. But the pain and the grief were too much for her. Seeking seclusion, Drusilla knelt down and poured out her heart, as only a mother would understand, to a loving God. She told the Lord He could take her oldest son if He wanted, "but please—please Lord, spare his life."

And then with that "peace that passeth all understanding," the Lord spoke to this woman of awesome faith. Gently and reassuringly, He said, "It shall be done unto you as it was unto Abraham when he offered Isaac on the altar." (Story based on "Historical Sketch of James Hendricks and Drusilla Dorris Hendricks," Typescript, LDS Church Archives.)

My dear friends, true religion requires sacrifice, or it will never produce strong faith. We of this pampered generation need not worry about whose sacrifices were greater, the pioneers' or ours. For the faithful, a just and loving Father in Heaven will make sure that the sacrifices and trials we endure are sufficient for the glory we will receive. But please know this: Those of us who are fond of our comfort and ease must understand there must be a price paid for faith.

It was once said this way: "No cross, no crown; No gall, no glory; No thorns, no throne" (President Ezra Taft Benson, Area Conference Report, Taipei, Taiwan, 1975, p. 3).

THE PALSIED MAN
AND HIS FRIENDS

It seems like these days when I kneel down to pray, the faces of a lot of people that I care about who are in trouble come to my mind, and a lot of my time in prayer is spent for them, hoping beyond hope that Heavenly Father will bless them because of my meager faith and my great concern. I'm sure it's the same with you.

But do you sometimes find yourself wondering if your prayers are doing any good? Will He really help them just because you ask Him to? Is He really listening? Are your feeble efforts with them and with Him making any difference at all?

If you have ever asked any of these questions, consider the following story.

On one of those rare occasions when the Master was at home in Capernaum, word spread quickly throughout the community that He was there, and a crowd came together—so large a crowd, in fact, that they filled His house to overflowing. To those close enough to hear, which evidently was not all, Jesus taught the gospel.

Four men were seen approaching the house carrying a sort of portable bed, upon which lay a man who was paralyzed. They tried to enter the house and get to Jesus, but they could not because of the crowd. Selflessly determined, these four men hefted their helpless friend up onto the flat roof of the house and tore the roof apart, creating a hole. Then they lowered their friend through the hole right into the middle of the crowd near Jesus. With compassion, Jesus bade the man to be of good cheer, forgave his sins, and healed his paralysis.

What impresses me most about this story is a little detail that Matthew, Mark, and Luke all record (see Matthew 9:2; Mark 2:1–5; Luke 5:18–20).

Mark's words were, "When Jesus saw their faith . . ." (Mark 2:5)— not "his faith," but "their faith."

In other words, we have here a man in the spiritual bondage of sin and the physical bondage of paralysis, who is healed—yes, by his own faith, but in great measure by the faith and the determination of those who loved him and were willing to sacrifice for him.

The next time you wonder if your pitiful prayers are doing any good, please remember this statement from the Apostle Paul: "the effectual fervent prayer of a righteous man availeth much" (James 5:16). And so it does.

God bless you. Don't ever give up!

WHEN YOU BELIEVE

A re there times when your faith and belief just aren't quite what you'd like them to be? Maybe there's something you need to believe in. May I share the story of one young woman?

How much more could one young woman's life be shattered than was Mary's at that moment? The final days of her senior year in high school should have been filled with joy, excitement, and anticipation of the future—but not now.

Two days before, Mary had come home from school. Her parents had gathered the family around the table for a grim announcement: Mother had cancer!

Mary had cried herself to sleep that night. And now, with the family again gathered around the table, the results of the most recent tests were even more devastating. The cancer had spread throughout her body.

Hiding her emotions, Mary prepared dinner for the family and got ready to go to work. Just before she went out the door, she stopped—and she gave her mother a hug.

Four years before, Mary's mother had battled cancer and won. Then, with the simple faith of a pure child, Mary had asked God to save her mother's life, and He had answered that prayer. But would He now? There had been no such assurance, though there had been many, many heartrending prayers.

Mary climbed into the car to go to work. Difficult questions raced through her mind. What if Mother died? What would the family do? What would she do? How could she go on without her mother? It was too much to bear. Mary began to cry. In an effort to direct her thoughts elsewhere, Mary turned on the radio.

As she listened, she recognized the final chorus of a familiar, popular song. The words captured her attention, and she listened until the song ended. Mary switched stations. Strangely enough, the same song was just beginning on the other station. This time as Mary listened, the power of the song reached deep into her heart. She heard these lyrics:

"Now we are not afraid, even though we have much to fear."

Something not of this world began to envelop Mary.

"It felt as though Heavenly Father put His arms around me," she said. "I fell into His arms."

"I can't do this!" she cried.

A feeling of intense love and comfort that could only be described as a heavenly embrace filled her whole being.

A voice seemed to speak to her mind, saying, "Mary, don't be afraid. I'll be with you the whole way. Trust me. I only want what's best for you."

Her tears of pain became cleansing tears of relief.

Words from the second verse seemed to strike a resounding chord in her heart:

"With hearts so full I can't explain it . . ." she heard.

The expressions of the artists were the emotions of her heart.

A change came over Mary from that moment forward. She was at peace. She didn't know what was going to happen—but it didn't matter. No matter what it is, life will go on. There will be happiness, there will be joy, and she won't be alone. That she does know!

Eighteen months later, Mary's mother quietly passed away surrounded by her family. It was not the miracle Mary had hoped for, but her mother outlived the doctors' predictions, even recovering just long enough to nurse Mary through her own health crisis.

Oh, God is good! He will not do anything to us that is not for our good. So what good could possibly come of such an ordeal? Listen to the courage of Mary's words:

"No matter what life may give me, I know if I have total trust in God, everything will be okay. I'm not alone, and I will never stop believing."

"There can be miracles when you believe.

Though hope is frail, it's hard to kill.

Who knows what miracles you can achieve

When you believe? Somehow you will.

Now you will; you will when you believe."

*From an experience of Mary West, May 1999. Lyrics from "When You Believe," Michelle Pfeiffer/Sally Dworsky, *The Prince of Egypt *original soundtrack.*

NICKNAMES

J esus is our Savior. Now, if all there was to His being our Savior was His redeeming sacrifice, then the Savior's work ended nearly two thousand years ago. But I want you to know that such is not the case; His redeeming work is not done. He is still involved in our lives. One of the reasons that Jesus is our Savior is because of His ability to see the divine in each one of us that we cannot see, and the ability through His love to bring it out. Consider John, chapter 1, when the Savior first meets Simon Peter.

Andrew brings Simon to meet the Savior. When the Savior sees Simon, He says to him, "Thou art Simon the son of Jona: thou shalt be called Cephas," or *Peter* in the Greek, "which is by interpretation, [a seer or] A stone" (John 1:42).

Can you imagine what those words must have done for Peter? One minute you are Simon, a lowly Galilean fisherman, and the next, you are a fisher of men, a personal friend of the Messiah, a seer, the greatest calling a man can have, and a man of rock! Surely, Peter would never have forgotten those words. Like a beacon before his soul, he would follow them and spend the rest of his life living up to them.

Look at the nickname the Master gave two of His other Apostles, James and John. He called them "Boanerges," which means—and I love this—"The sons of thunder" (Mark 3:17).

We all have things about ourselves we want to change. But I have found, and so have you, that it is so much easier to change when we have a friend to help us. The Savior is that friend. From the first moment we begin to become acquainted with Him, we feel the gentle but firm upward tug of His love and faith. He will not rest until He has drawn forth from us every talent, every virtue, and every power lying latent within us that we will give Him. And so it is.

ALLELOPATHY

It was about twenty-five years ago on a field trip in the deserts of Utah that I first learned of this interesting phenomenon of nature. We were studying juniper trees, and it was pointed out to me that no grass ever grows in close proximity to Utah Juniper. It is not because grass and juniper compete for resources and the juniper wins. Rather, it is because of something called *allelopathy*.

In the simplest of terms, *allelopathy* means that juniper trees exude something into the soil around them that kills or inhibits the growth of other plants. Juniper forests are not like pine forests, where the trees are thick and close together and the understory is rife with vegetation. Juniper trees stand by themselves.

Juniper is not the only plant that does this. There are many. Black walnut trees are one of the most powerful. They don't just inhibit some plants; they kill every plant around them by the chemicals they give off. They are indeed a toxic neighbor.

Of course, this is not a botany lesson. Jesus once said, "Be of good cheer." (John 16:33). May I illustrate why that is so important?

When we do not obey that commandment, we practice spiritual allelopathy. When we are negative, grumpy, angry, or moody, we radiate that toxicity to those around us, effectively killing or inhibiting any and all affections we might receive. If we persist, we may find ourselves standing all alone in an emotional desert of our own creation.

It is so much better, figuratively speaking, to live in a jungle, where all want to be close, even symbiotic—sharing, living, and loving life together. Hence, the conclusion of this story might well be, away with the toxicity of sourfaced picklesuckers!

TEACHING,
A SACRED TRUST

One summer more than thirty years ago, I was hired by a neighbor to tend a small band of sheep. My job was to take them to the mountain pastures each day, watch them, and then bring them safely home that night. I had been strictly warned when I took the job to not let the sheep stray too near the alfalfa fields, or they'd break through and bloat on the rich feed.

One day, though, I carelessly let the sheep get too near the fence, and they broke through. The entire band quickly spread across the field and began gorging themselves. I panicked. I ran around screaming and waving my arms, desperately trying to drive the sheep out, but it did no good at all. They melted around me like water and went on eating.

Finally, the owner and his son came. As they hurried past me to save the sheep, one of them said something to me about the instructions I had ignored. It angered me, and in a rage, I turned and ran—not toward the sheep, but away from them. I ran all the way home. At that moment, I could not have cared less if every last one of those sheep died. Fortunately, though, none of them did.

That experience has come back to me often. I've since learned that a teacher is a shepherd. Teaching is the Savior's own profession, and His is the art of shepherding the lambs of God to the pastures of truth, no matter whether that pasture is religion, science, mathematics, or anything else. Truth is truth, no matter where it's found! And teaching is a sacred trust.

Speaking as a father, may God bless those teachers who touch the lives of the children. And someday, teachers, who's to say how grateful those lambs will be for you, and for all those who guided them safely to pasture and brought them back home?

KIDNEY STONES

One night not long ago after a late-night family movie, my little boy Adam crawled in bed with me wanting a bedtime story. I was just a few pages into *Beauty and the Beast* when all of a sudden, a pain hit me in the back and began to intensify. Within moments it was so bad I couldn't breathe. When I sat up, it felt as though someone had stuck a knife in my back. I knew what it was; I'd heard of it before. It was a kidney stone.

My wife and daughters got me to the hospital, and I have to tell you I've known pain in my life, but I have never known pain like that! The hospital hooked me up to IVs and began to pump me full of painkillers. Oh, they were wonderful! I still remember that feeling. One of these was Toradol.

If I had known what this drug would do to me, I would never have gotten within a hundred yards of it. Now, while I languished in the hospital, the kidney stone refused to move. So, the hospital personnel naturally increased the fluid drip into my body in an attempt to flush the stone out. I don't know how many bottles of that stuff went into me.

By late Sunday night, the stone was still there, as was the pain, and something was definitely wrong with my body. None of the fluid going in was coming out. Toradol had shut down my kidneys. By the time I left the hospital for home, I resembled the Pillsbury Dough Boy, and the stone was still there!

The words *retaining water* took on a completely new meaning for me. None of my clothes fit. It was so bad that even sweatpants were tight. I lost sight of my feet for the first time in my life; I couldn't even bend over. For the next several days, whenever I lay down to sleep, I felt as though I was being hung upside down. When I climbed on the scales, I discovered that in my 36 hours in the hospital, I had gained more than 30 pounds, and I only weigh 150 pounds dripping wet!

At one point, I came downstairs, utterly appalled at my awful appearance. I said to my wife and my oldest daughter, "Look at this!"

I pulled up my sweatshirt and grabbed my more-than-ample stomach and shook it! It jiggled and rolled like a giant bowl of unset Jell-O. It was disgusting! They thought it was hilarious; they still do.

My wife, having borne seven children, made some comment in the midst of her gales of laughter like, "Well, now you know what pregnancy feels like, don't you?"

I don't recall ever really wanting to know what pregnancy felt like.

Well, I went to my doctor, who's a good friend. He was a little surprised at what had happened to me; I guess Toradol was not supposed to do that. He said, "Well, we need to get your kidneys going again."

He gave me some pills, and oh, did they work! Over the next four days I lost the entire thirty pounds plus more, underwent surgery for the stone, and painfully passed two more stones. When it was over, my body felt like it had spent a week in a washer—on the spin cycle!

Why do I tell you all of that? Because knowledge is power. What we don't know can hurt us, just like what I didn't know hurt me. Our agency is only as good as our knowledge. The more we know of truth, the stronger our agency, the more choices we have, and thus the more power we have over our lives.

What you don't know limits your ability to choose and allows you to be deceived. If only I had known that my troubles could likely have been prevented by a few extra ounces of water each day! Most of our troubles in life could be solved by a few extra minutes of living water—the Word of the Lord studied and applied.

Again, experience taught me that taking Toradol and being pumped full of IV fluid has terrible consequences. If only I had known.

Don't let experience teach you about guilt, pain, and hell. Remember, knowledge is power. Ignorance and stupidity are not bliss; they're bondage! May we stand in the light of the Lord Jesus Christ and never be moved.

RACHEL AND ADRIAN

I remember a line from a movie that was produced years ago that had a powerful, even a life-changing impact on me. The line was, "No one can make it happily through this life and into the next without the Savior."

I've thought a lot about that line. How do we go out and lay hold upon the kind of happiness that this speaks of in a world that's so full of opposition? And why is it that the most seasoned and mature of the Savior's disciples are the ones who love life the most, even while they are often the ones simultaneously bearing the most difficult burdens?

Well, there's a quality about these people, and perhaps this story will illustrate what that quality is.

Rachel first met Adrian in October 1994 on, of all places, a blind date. They spent a wonderful weekend together—sparks flying, as you can imagine—attending church meetings. There was something about this young man who loved the Lord so much that interested her. Their next date was again to a sacred church experience. By December, that interest between the two of them had transformed into an eternal love. And then on Christmas Eve, Adrian gave Rachel a significantly wrapped Christmas gift. Rachel opened it, and inside was a book entitled *Just for Newlyweds*. It was his proposal; what a way to ask!

They were married in June 1995, excited at the prospects of beginning a whole new life together. Two years later, they graduated from college. Adrian then enrolled in a master's program in physical therapy. One year after they were married, Mason came along, adding a sweeter dimension to their marriage. Then three years after that, Carter was born. "He was the greatest dad," Rachel said.

"He was always playing with his boys, wrestling, playing basketball, tickling them." Rachel described coming home on more than one occasion and finding Adrian on the sofa, curled up with Mason in his arms, both of them taking a nap together. Life was wonderful.

After two long years, Adrian's graduation neared. He was excited to begin work as a physical therapist. But it was right about this time that he noticed a nagging pain in his side. Doctors initially diagnosed it as gastritis, but the pain didn't go away.

The day after Adrian finished school—he was all done—he woke up very sick. This time Rachel knew something was terribly wrong when the doctor called them in, pulled his chair right up next to them, and announced, "Cancer—pancreatic cancer." They gave him a 5 percent chance of survival. "They never gave us any hope," Rachel said.

Within two weeks, Adrian underwent radical surgery. He recovered from that, but never completely. Over the next ten months, Adrian deteriorated steadily, until he was little more than an emaciated shell. But those ten months were in some ways glorious. It was just Adrian, Rachel, Mason, and Carter, all day, every day, together as a family. There were many late-night talks between Adrian and Rachel, planning and preparing for the future—how to raise the boys after he was gone.

Then one morning, Rachel awoke, and Adrian was gone. Significantly, more than we understand now, Adrian left this life on Easter morning, April 23, 2000.

Now I ask you, is this cruel and unfair to leave Rachel, a twenty-six-year-old widow with two little boys to raise alone? Some would say it is, but not if you ask her. She's not alone. There is something about this young woman, an infectious cheerfulness and optimism that radiates from her like a light. When I asked her about it, she said it was her goal to be happy, to be pleasant.

"I want Adrian," she said, "to look down and see me happy."

How could anyone be happy and cheerful under such trying circumstances? I believe I found the answer when I went to her home. If you go into Rachel's home, there are several pictures hanging prominently around the family room; most of them are photographs of the family, including Adrian. But there is one portrait occupying the central place in the room. It is of the Lord Jesus Christ, He who once said, "I am the way, the truth, and the life" (John 14:6); "he that believeth in me, though he were dead, yet shall he live" (John 11:25). This is what makes Rachel the way she is.

My friends, faith is not just to believe in Christ and that He's out there—somewhere. It is to believe Christ, and that He will be there, that He will keep His promises to us. When we believe in Christ in that way, that is called faith. And when faith is there, hope is born within us that beckons us to follow Him, counting on His promises. That hope is now an anchoring force holding Rachel and her boys steady and serene on the straight and narrow path.

Listen to this prayer that her little boy Mason offered not long ago: "Heavenly Father, please help Daddy to be happy in heaven. We're thankful that the gospel is so true, and that we can be a family forever if we live righteously."

To be hopeless is to be homeless. Look at your life. If your hope has dimmed or disappeared, come unto Christ as the little child and find it again. Life can be glorious in spite of it all.

Experience of Rachel Cook.

PRAYER

Question for you: What is the most often-commanded commandment in all of the scriptures—perhaps one of the most persistent themes in all of the revelations? It is the commandment to pray.

Many years ago, a couple went to see their spiritual leader. Their teenage son had left home one night and never returned. He had been gone for several weeks. The parents were stricken with grief and came for help.

"Have you pleaded with the Lord to know where he is?" their leader asked.

They assured him that they had.

"Have you pleaded with all your strength?" he persisted.

"Yes, we have," they said.

Still, he pressed them, "Have you pleaded with every particle of your being?"

Well, they admitted that perhaps they had not prayed with quite that much intent.

"You go home and pray with every particle and strength of your being," he said.

They said they would, and they left his office. Six o'clock that night the phone rang. It was their son calling from several hundred miles away in Canada. Relieved, they visited with him and assured themselves that he was safe and in no danger. Then it occurred to them to ask why he had called at that particular time.

"The bishop came over to my apartment this evening," he said. "He had the strongest impression to have me call home, and he said he would not leave until I did."

Well, that story impressed me when I read it, and I felt inclined to share it with you. But there's a second part to that story that makes it even more compelling.

In 1943, at the height of World War II, that spiritual leader who counseled those parents was just a boy. One Sunday just before Thanksgiving, he attended church services with his older brother. Twice during the meetings, the members of that ward were asked to not let that Thanksgiving pass without kneeling down as a family and thanking God for His goodness and their many blessings. Well, as Vaughn went home that night, there welled up in his little-boy heart a powerful, overwhelming desire to follow that counsel and have family prayer. But that would take some doing. Mom was not a Church member, and Dad was an alcoholic. Prayers were not said in their home.

Monday, Tuesday, Wednesday—it consumed Vaughn's thoughts. How could he get his family to have family prayer? Finally, Thanksgiving Day arrived. Vaughn skipped breakfast that morning so that he would have a greater appetite. He and his brothers went outside and entertained themselves digging a hole, but as his hunger increased, so greater did his appetite for prayer. It was all he could think of. He wanted it more than the meal itself. But did he have the courage to ask?

At 2:30 that afternoon, Mom called the family together. There spread before them was the sumptuous feast they had been waiting for. It was now or never. Vaughn's heart felt about to burst. *Please,* he thought, *won't someone suggest that we have a family prayer?* But he couldn't get the words to come out. He didn't dare.

The food was being passed around the table, and plates were being filled. Vaughn looked at his older brother, who had been in the same meeting, praying desperately that he would say something. Time was running out. And then everyone began to eat, just like always. It was too late. His heart sank and despair filled his soul. In spite of a great hunger and wonderful food, he had no appetite. He didn't want the food. He wanted to pray.

Well, then and there, Vaughn vowed that no son or daughter of his would ever want to pray and not be able to. Prayer became a bulwark to Vaughn Featherstone for the rest of his life.

In the New Testament, Jesus gave two parables regarding prayer. The first was called "The friend at midnight," and the second was "The parable of the unjust judge." These are unique parables. They're not parables of comparison, as usual. But they are powerful parables of contrast. God is more willing and eager to answer our prayers than often we are to ask. And further, we pray with all the energy of our soul not to change the will of God, but to change our spiritual position so that we may know the will of God. Maybe it's time to pray.

Adapted from Vaughn J. Featherstone, "Thanksgiving Prayer," New Era, November 1985, 7.

TRUST THE PILOT

A couple of years ago, my wife and I flew with a pilot friend of ours and his wife to Sun Valley for a dinner date. Our plan was to fly over and come back that night. It was my first flight in a single-engine small aircraft, and my friend, Jerry, had only had his license a couple of months.

As we returned, the view from high above the Arco desert was magnificent. It seemed as though we could see forever in all directions, and the stars overhead were beautiful. Even now it's difficult to describe what that was like.

As we approached our hometown, Jerry commented that he couldn't see the airport runway marker lights in the darkness. His comment brought all of us to full attention. The chatter in the cockpit was instantly silenced, replaced by a keen sense of fear and nervous tension; we were scared!

We approached and circled the town, but the lights were nowhere to be seen. We would have to land in the dark.

It didn't seem to me at the time that I had a lot of options. I could panic and become a screaming idiot, I could take over the controls of the airplane, or I could open the door and jump out. None of those options seemed very appealing at the time. For the first time in recent memory, I considered that I might die. Then, Jerry looked at me, and with a calm, confident demeanor, he said, "Don't worry. Trust me."

Something in what he said and the way he said it spoke peace to me, and I was no longer afraid; I felt calm.

Jerry circled and brought the plane down where he thought the runway should be. In spite of my assurance, it was still a tense moment watching the blackness of the earth rush toward us. It turned out that we were slightly east of the runway as the plane's lights hit the ground. But with a quick, skillful maneuver, the plane's course was corrected, and we landed without mishap. I don't know if I have ever been so grateful to put my feet back on the earth.

Later I reflected on the experience. It seems that our lives are like that plane flight. We are all flying in a darkened world, and it's too late to turn back. We're in the air; we're committed. The only choice we have is to see the flight through to the end. And when we get ourselves into trouble, as we all do, some of us are tempted to quit, to bail out, and to end it all. Others of us arrogantly try to take over the controls. But both solutions have the same eternal consequence—misery and further pain.

There is a better way, one that will bring peace and happiness, and one that leaves us free to enjoy the experience and the incredible views that will be opened to us.

That solution is simple: Trust the pilot. Let Him take over the controls, and not only will we arrive at our heavenly destination, but by the grace of God, we will have had a grand and glorious adventure.

TOM

Sometimes what we most need in this difficult world is a friend, someone whose encouragement is constant, who won't coddle us, but who won't let us be beaten up either. May I share an example of what I mean?

It was a warm, summer afternoon. Tom was out on the back patio of his Las Vegas home when he heard shouting and angry voices from inside the house. As he entered, he saw one of his teenage sons pitting his stubborn will against the determined correction of his mother. Tom's desire was to calm the situation and reconcile his loved ones. But within minutes he was drawn into the melee and was shouting worse than the other two. Well, it wasn't long before mother and son stormed out in opposite directions, leaving Tom standing there.

He felt terrible. He returned to the patio; shame and guilt washed over him. He had only wanted to help, but instead he'd made the situation worse. Right there on the patio, Tom knelt down and began to pray—praying for forgiveness, acknowledging his pride and his unbecoming behavior, and asking that peace and a healing spirit be poured out on his wife and son.

And then it happened. It was as clear as if it were audibly spoken. A voice out of eternity echoed in Tom's mind. "Father, Tom has done it again! But he wants to do good. For Me, please grant the petitions of his prayer."

Tom said, "I marveled. It was so personal. With countless people on the earth, the Father and the Savior were attentive to me in that moment. I knew with certainty the Master had somehow reached into that infinite reserve He had earned in Gethsemane and paid the price that unalterable justice required. And I was free of pain of heart."

Now the sense of their forgiveness was real and soothing for Tom. Within a few minutes, that same Spirit moved upon his wife and son. They came together; apologies were shared, and a healing was affected. Harmony and peace were restored once more to their home.

Oh, my friends, the Savior is our Advocate and our truest Friend. If we will let Him, He will not only stand between us and justice, but also between us and a world that seeks to bully and destroy us. Even our own weaknesses and fears will eventually give way to the power of our omnipotent friend. Thank God for the gift of His Son, the gift of the truest of friends.

Adapted from Thomas L. Tyler, The Savior—Our Friend and Advocate.

THOU ART THE CHRIST

I don't think it would be too bold to say that more rumors, legends, and traditions have been perpetuated about the Savior of the world than any modern celebrity ever dreamed of. Every conceivable notion has been advanced to explain who He was and what He was. I have lost track how many times His Second Coming has occurred, according to supermarket tabloids. The more things change, the more things stay the same.

Sometime in the second year of the Savior's ministry, Jesus and His Apostles went off alone. As they went, Jesus asked them, "Whom do men say that I the Son of Man am?" (Matthew 16:13).

The Apostles answered according to the rumors circulating among the people at that time, "Some say . . . thou art John the Baptist," they said, "some, Elias; . . . others, Jeremias, or one of the prophets" (Matthew 16:14).

You see, rumor had it among the Jews that Jesus was John the Baptist come back to life after being killed by Herod. Even Herod believed that. Still others believed that Jesus was Elijah, the great prophet taken to heaven without tasting death, whom the scriptures promised would return before the great and dreadful day of the Lord. And still others superstitiously believed that Jesus was Jeremias or another of the prophets reincarnated. It seems that rumors are always more popular than the truth.

Then Jesus asked them, "But whom say ye that I am? And Simon Peter answered and said, Thou art the Christ, the Son of the living God" (Matthew 16:15–16).

Peter had received revelation from God, and so must we. Until we do, until we know what Peter knew, Jesus's identity and importance will always remain a matter of doubt to us and a source of weakness. For a doubting and cynical world, perhaps the great Christian philosopher C. S. Lewis put it best. He said:

I am trying here to prevent anyone saying the really foolish thing that people often say about Him: [That is] "I'm ready to accept Jesus as a great moral teacher, but I don't accept His claim to be God." That is the one thing we must not say. A man who was merely a man and said the sort of things Jesus said would not be a great moral teacher. He would either be a lunatic—on a level with the man who says he is a poached egg—or else he would be the devil of Hell. You must make your choice. Either this man was, and is, the son of God; or else a madman or something worse. You can shut him up for a fool, you can spit at him and kill him as a demon; or you can fall at His feet and call Him Lord and God. But let us not come with any patronizing nonsense about His being a great human teacher. He has not left that open to us. He did not intend to. (*Mere Christianity* [New York: Macmillan Publishing Co., 1952], 40–41)

THE VISION OF ENOCH

There are a lot of people on this earth. Have you ever asked yourself, *How in the world can God keep track of all of us? I mean, let alone love us and hear us? There are quite a few of us.* Well, if you've ever wondered about that, please consider this touching story recorded by Moses from the life of Enoch the prophet.

After Enoch built his remarkable city called Zion, Enoch received a vision in which he saw that Zion would eventually be taken up into heaven, leaving behind those people who, for the most part, had not chosen righteousness. Enoch is then permitted to see nation after nation of these people, some of whom repent and are saved, but most of whom continue in wickedness. Then Enoch sees Satan laughing with a great chain in his hand veiling the whole face of the earth in darkness.

Right after Enoch sees Satan laughing because of the wickedness of men, he sees this interesting thing: Enoch sees God weeping. He is evidently surprised, and he asks, "How is it that the heavens weep, and shed forth their tears as rain upon the mountains?" (Moses 7:28). "How is it that thou canst weep, seeing thou art holy, and from all eternity to all eternity? And were it possible that man could number the particles of the earth, yea, millions of earths like this, it would not be a beginning to the number of thy creations; and thy curtains are stretched out still; and yet"—now listen carefully—"thou art there, and thy bosom is there; and [also] thou art just; thou art merciful and kind forever" (Moses 7:29–30).

Even in the asking, Enoch's question is an incredible revelation. With an infinity of worlds and children, even with all of that, the

God of the universe is here for us; His heart is here, His tears are here, and He is merciful and kind forever. When God's children suffer, no matter where they are, especially if it's unnecessary, He suffers with them, even to tears.

You know, there may be nearly six billion people on this earth, but that's okay. When you know that the eye of God is upon you, and the heart and soul of God are with you, it no longer matters how many others there are or where they are. It becomes as though you were the only one.

Adapted from Moses 7, Pearl of Great Price.

MITCHIE

I am convinced that we are not alone in this world. There is a loving power that knows us, that watches over us, and that guides us if we'll listen, as this story that is so very close to home illustrates.

A few months ago, my brother-in-law Shayne had an experience that even now in the telling fills his eyes with tears and his heart with deep gratitude.

Late one night well after his children were all down in bed, he made his way to his second-floor bedroom. As he passed by the top of the stairs, however, he noticed a light on downstairs in the kitchen. Knowing that the family was all in bed and that all the lights should be off, he paused, puzzled, and asked his wife if she had left any lights on. She answered that she hadn't. He contemplated the long journey down the stairs to turn it off, but fatigue won out; he decided to leave it on and go to bed.

Having made that decision, he started to turn toward his bedroom when he was stopped by a gentle impression that he should investigate further. He nearly ignored it—sleep was calling more loudly, but the feeling persisted.

Without a second thought, he descended the stairs. As he rounded the corner into the kitchen, he discovered Mitchie, his two-and-a-half-year-old son, up in the middle of the kitchen counter surrounded by two containers of high-potency medicine. Both caps were off, and a bright-pink ring circled the toddler's mouth.

Reacting quickly, the terrified father rushed the boy to the hospital, where competent medical personnel acted swiftly and saved his life.

You could never convince Shayne that he wasn't prompted by the God of heaven, not ever so long as he can look into the bright, vibrant eyes of that beloved son who will evermore serve as a continual reminder of the goodness of God.

Experience of Shayne Hemsley.

"He Cares"

It was the summer of 1962, and Lynette was in Paris, which would seem the dream of a lifetime for any nineteen-year-old young woman. She had worked hard to be there. She and others auditioned to be a part of a renowned symphonic band that would travel and perform across Europe. And not only was she chosen, but she was first chair.

Somewhere in the beginning of the trip from Utah to Paris, she began to feel the pangs of homesickness. But why? She had been off to college—away from home. No matter, why. It hurt—terribly.

On the day they were to tour the white cliffs of Dover in England, she experienced a migraine that kept her from sightseeing.

By the time she reached Paris, the homesickness was more than just a state of mind—it was a state of body as well. She cried out to God for comfort and help. She desperately wanted to go home but knew she could not. She just couldn't bear to be gone that long and that far away.

With her friends, Lynette went to the Eiffel Tower, and though awed by the very sight of it, the pain for her was still ever-present. They rode the elevators to the very top and experienced that breathtaking, once-in-a-lifetime view of the city. When they were done, they got into the elevator and descended to the middle level, where there would be a short wait for another elevator to take them to the ground.

As they stood there waiting, they heard the familiar beep signaling that the elevator door was about to open. The doors opened—and standing there, ready to step out, was her stake president, neighbor, and friend from back home. With a cry of relief and joy, Lynette launched herself into his arms. He held her and spoke words of comfort.

From that moment forward, the pain and homesickness were gone, and she was able to finish the tour, and—more importantly—to have fun. Nearly sixty years after the event, Lynette told me, "The Lord hears and answers our prayers. He cares about who, what, and where we are. If it matters to us, it matters to Him." And so it is!

LIFE ISN'T FAIR

Not too long ago on a beautiful spring day, I came home from work and found two of my daughters playing in the front yard. One of them didn't look too happy. I invited her to sit down with me on the front step and asked her what was wrong. She launched into a tirade as only a five-year-old can about how everything is so unfair and so hard, especially at kindergarten.

Oh, it was bad! The teacher had criticized her work, she couldn't sit with her favorite friend, her sister wouldn't play with her, her brother wouldn't wrestle with her, and on and on she went. She was having a bad day, and there was nothing I was going to say that was going to change that.

Suddenly I got an idea. Since I couldn't reason with her to help her feel better, maybe I could distract her.

"Look, Honey," I said, pointing to the sun that was just going down. "The sun's going behind the tree. Ah, now I won't get to see it anymore; I won't get to feel its warmth anymore. That is so unfair!"

She looked at me like I was kind of weird and said, "No, it's not!"

"Yes, it is," I argued. "Now I'll never get to see it again!"

"Yes, you will."

"No, I won't."

We argued back and forth, me pointing out the unfairness of the sun going down and her promising its return.

Finally, with great earnestness and some exasperation, she blurted out, "It's okay, Dad! The sun will come out again!"

I stopped and looked at her expectantly for a moment. But she didn't get it. Maybe she never will. No, she will—someday.

We went out for ice cream.

WHITEWASHED

In our daily struggle to overcome the big sins, once in a while it helps to remember the little ones too. So, I begin with a question: Where would we be if God got offended as often as some of us do?

Some time ago I was with a group of young friends. After several hours of intense meetings, we decided to get out of the cabin and have a good, old-fashioned football game, girls and all. Now picture if you can a dozen or so people bundled to the hilt in winter clothing in a tackle football game in several feet of snow. I was by far the old man of the group, but I joined in. On one of the first plays, I caught a pass and was instantly knocked off my feet into a snowdrift. They had no mercy for the old man.

Well, the game went on. The competition was fierce, and the hits were hard. The girls in the group tackled as hard as they got tackled. I'm sure all of us got our chimes rung a few times, but no one complained, and we had a good time. The most noteworthy thing to me was that no matter how hard they got hit or whitewashed in the snow, no one got angry—not even close.

At the conclusion of the game, as we were walking back to the cabin tired and cold, one of the guys who was still feeling rambunctious tackled one of the girls—and in spite of her protests, he buried her face deep in the snow. She came up spitting and sputtering! I thought she was going to hit him. He jumped up laughing, went after another girl, and similarly whitewashed her.

Just a few minutes later, one of the guys had stripped off all of his snow clothes and was standing on the porch in socks, gym shorts, and a tee shirt. Along came our problem child again and shoved him out into the deep snow, forcing him to do the cold-toe-two-step.

I watched all this with keen interest to see how my three wronged friends would react. Would they get offended? To my surprise and delight, none of the three got angry, and they had had more than sufficient provocation. But each of them—and I watched this—each of them made a decision to shake off not only the snow, but the anger. They chose to laugh, and they went on and forgot it.

In spite of fourteen hours together in cramped quarters with intense interaction, we were better friends at the end of the day than at the beginning. Why? This is a key—there was a lot of laughing, and no offense was taken.

Being offended is natural, but that's just it. It is of the natural man, not the divine man. If we want to, and by the grace of God, we may become quick to laugh, slow to anger, and a light unto the world. After all, getting offended is just like getting a head cold. It's just like what my grandmother used to say—it just makes snots out of people.

DADDY

The Psalmist said, "children are an heritage of the Lord" and "Happy is the man that hath [many] of them" (Psalms 127:3, 5).

Not long ago, I was sitting in a church meeting with my youngest daughter, my four-year-old, on my lap. The congregation was singing. My daughter, not terribly interested in singing, became fascinated with my pocket hymnal, which has my name embossed on the front.

She reached up and grabbed my head and pulled it down where she could speak in my ear.

"Daddy, whose name is that?"

"Well, that's my name, Honey. See," I said whispering, "Glenn Rawson."

My daughter is very matter of fact and minces no words.

"That's not your name!" she said.

"It—It's not?"

"No!"

Suddenly I was very curious to know who my daughter thought I was. So, I asked, "Well, then, what is my name?"

She didn't even hesitate. "It's Daddy!"

It's hard to describe how that statement tugged on my heart-strings, but it did. Still, I felt that she ought to know that all daddies have other names too.

So, I said, "Well, that's true, Honey, but I also have another name. It's Glenn Raw—"

"No!" she said firmly, cutting me off. "Your name is Daddy!"

I gave up trying to change her mind. I just smiled and hugged her. Since that time, the name *Daddy* has become more special to me. My hope is that as time goes on, she never becomes too old to think of me as her Daddy.

THE WEEPING
WOMAN

It seems to me that no one can truly love the Savior and know Him if they've never needed Him, as this story illustrates.

Early in the Savior's ministry, He was invited to the house of Simon the Pharisee, who seems, even in the invitation, motivated by an arrogant curiosity about the Master. When the Savior arrives at his home, Simon disdainfully neglects the usual social customs afforded an honored guest.

While the diners were reclining feet out on couches around the table, a woman enters and stands at the feet of the Savior. Without a word, she falls at His feet weeping and begins kissing His feet, bathing them with her tears and wiping them with her hair.

Simon, knowing something of the woman's sinful reputation, scorns the Master in His thoughts and watches the proceedings with contempt. Discerning those sin-darkened thoughts, Jesus defends the woman's actions and rebukes the self-righteous, judgmental Pharisee, teaching him with penetrating clarity, "to whom little is forgiven, the same loveth little" (Luke 7:47).

To the penitent, grateful woman, and with tender mercy, the Master declares, "Thy sins are forgiven" (Luke 7:48). "Thy faith hath saved thee; go in peace" (Luke 7:50).

When our love and faith in the Savior of the world drives us weeping to our knees seeking His power to forgive, we too can then come to truly love Him and know something of the joy of "mercy's arms."

ORANGE JUICE

It seems like whenever I get into a conversation with people about popular movies, there's a line that always goes something like this: "Oh, there's just that one little part you have to worry about—but other than that, it's a great movie!"

You ever heard that line? To me, that's an instant danger signal—there's something wrong. In regard to movies like that, I have a story.

One Sunday afternoon, we were just finishing our family dinner when somehow the conversation turned to popular movies. One of my daughters mentioned a very popular movie that had one of those very objectionable scenes in it. And she said something like this: "Dad, what's so wrong with that movie? I'd really like to see it. We can always fast-forward through that two-minute part."

She knew about the bad part in that movie. She knew it was wrong, but the rest of the movie had captured her imagination, and she wanted to see it.

Therein lies the problem. People's taste in music and movies is an extension of what's in their hearts. So to criticize their movies or their music is to criticize them, and they take it personally.

Instead of arguing with my daughter, I remembered something a friend of mine had done in a class. Sitting on the table was a pitcher of orange juice with just one cup left in the bottom. I poured that last cup, held it up, and asked her if she wanted it. My children love orange juice, and of course she wanted it.

"Okay then," I said, "follow me."

With most of my children curiously following, I took the glass of orange juice and walked into the bathroom. I reached into the toilet with another cup and dipped out some toilet water. Ever so carefully, I poured just one tiny drop of toilet water into the orange juice.

I held it out to her. "Here you go," I said.

She screamed! And she ran out of the bathroom.

"But, Honey," I said as I held it out to her, "It's only one little drop."

"I don't care!" she yelled. "It's yucky!"

You know, I could not get her to come within ten feet of that glass of orange juice. I finally had to pour it out, and—well, you know where.

Since that time, I have not had a single argument with any of my children about which movies they should be watching. I hope I never have to.

The prophet Isaiah once said, "… be ye clean, that bear the vessels of the Lord" (Isaiah 52:11).

THE MARATHON

Family and family relationships are as vital to complete and lasting happiness as is water to an ocean.

Not too long ago, I decided that on my next birthday, I would run a marathon. I don't know why; call me stupid. I just wanted to see if I could do it. I had no desire to run a formally organized marathon. I wanted to do this all by myself, just to see if I could. It was then that I discovered that it was just the right distance to run from my front door to the LDS temple, a little more than twenty-six miles—perfect!

At 4:45 a.m. on the appointed day, all stretched out and ready to go, I left my house and started running. The first thirteen miles went quite smoothly, but at about mile eighteen, I "hit the wall"! My legs felt like lead; it felt as though my feet were one big, hypersensitive nerve and that my toenails were being torn off. I seriously began to wonder if I could make it to the end.

I'd had only about a month and a half to train for this marathon. But during that time, I watched my children get excited about my goal. Sometimes they even went running with me. If I stopped now, how would I face them and explain failure? I couldn't. I pushed on. I have never felt such concentrated, intense pain, especially self-inflicted.

I kept promising myself as I ran that I would stop and rest when I reached this or that goal, but for some reason, I kept going when I reached that goal. Around mile twenty-five, when I was moving slowly but still moving, my family drove past me hollering and screaming on their way to the temple. I was so glad I was still running.

At one point, just a couple of blocks shy of the temple, I got stopped by traffic. Not even a goal is worth getting run over. When

I finally got across the street and tried to run again, I couldn't. I couldn't make my legs work; it hurt too badly!

Then, more staggering than running, I rounded the last corner and saw my family standing at the temple's southwest corner with a ribbon stretched across the sidewalk. At that same moment I heard my son shout, "C'mon, Dad!"

It's hard to describe how those words hit me. They went deeper into me than he'll ever know in this life. I was overwhelmed with a feeling of love and gratitude for my family.

Suddenly this marathon became something more than a feeble man's goal. It became something eternal; it became a microcosm of life. I saw my wonderful little family standing on the soil of eternity, cheering me on as I struggled to endure the pain of finishing the most grueling race I had ever run, the race against myself. Sobbing and gasping for air, I crossed their little tape with not even enough strength to pull it out of their hands. Instantly, they surrounded me, hugging and congratulating me; I couldn't even talk. The crowning moment came when they pinned a gaudy, little, homemade ribbon on my chest that read *Number-One Dad*.

My dear friends, the marathon of a righteous mortality will be the toughest experience we will ever face as eternal beings. A wise and knowing Father knew it would be, and thus gave us a fan club, people to support us and cheer us on—a family. I believe that as we strive to faithfully finish life's race, we are loved, watched, and cheered on by family on both sides of the veil. And when our race is run and we finally cross that line, we will gratefully fall into the arms of an anxious and loving family to whom we are "number one."

After all, who would ever want to go into eternity without his or her family?

The Lord bless you.

STATE TROOPER

I have a few questions for you, and I want you to really think about them. What kind of a father is God? How does He work with His children? What's His style of discipline? Well, I hope this story will illustrate a point related to those questions.

Not long ago, I was driving across a busy Idaho highway in a truck. It was a beautiful morning, and I was thoroughly enjoying the drive. Part of that particular highway is posted with a fifty-five-mile-per-hour speed limit. The other part is sixty-five. I thought I was on the sixty-five-mile-per-hour part. I wasn't, but I was driving like I was.

There I was, clipping along, taking in the scenery, enjoying the day, and just loving life, when suddenly I passed an Idaho state trooper. I didn't give him much thought. I mean, why should I? I was legal—wasn't I? No sooner had I passed him than my CB radio came to life, causing me to jump.

"Hey, Handy," a deep voice said.

"Yes," I answered.

"You're going sixty-nine miles per hour."

I laughed nervously. "Yes." I knew who it was.

And then he said with kind of a drawl, "You have an extra $53 you don't know what to do with?"

"No," I said. "I'll keep it."

"Fifty-five will do just fine," he said firmly.

"Okay, thank you."

Then you could almost see the grin on this officer's face as he added, "You owe me."

"That I do," I said, "that I do." And I went on my way down the road, relieved and chuckling to myself. And I obeyed that speed limit for the rest of the day.

That state trooper could have really taken it to me. He had every right. I was clearly in the wrong; I was breaking the law. He could have pulled me over, chewed me out, inspected my rig, cited me, and a host of other things if he'd wanted to. But he didn't. And at least for me, he didn't have to; it wasn't necessary. I'm pretty conscientious about obeying traffic laws. All I needed was a gentle reminder.

None of us is perfect. All of us break the laws of God. And if God wanted to, He could be pretty harsh. In fact, He could be *really* harsh! But He's not that way. For those of us who are trying, He doesn't need to be. His style of discipline doesn't do radical surgery when a hug and a Band-Aid will do just fine. He's kind, He's gentle, and He's persistently persuasive with reminders. In fact, a line from a hymn comes to mind, and to me it says everything about the parenting style of Heavenly Father. It says, "How gentle God's commands. How kind His precepts are" ("How Gentle God's Commands," No. 125, *Hymns*, Salt Lake City: The Church of Jesus Christ of Latter-day Saints).

THE CHRISTMAS STORY

No stories we can tell have nearly as much power on the human heart as the words of the scriptures themselves. Would you permit me to share the Christmas story with you as related by Luke?

"And it came to pass in those days, that there went out a decree from Caesar Augustus, that all the world should be taxed. (And this taxing was first made when Cyrenius was governor of Syria.) And all went to be taxed, every one into his own city. And Joseph also went up from Galilee, out of the city of Nazareth, into Judaea, unto the city of David, which is called Bethlehem; (because he was of the house and lineage of David:) To be taxed with Mary his espoused wife, being great with child" (Luke 2:1–5).

"And so it was, that, while they were there, the days were accomplished that she should be delivered. And she brought forth her firstborn son, and wrapped him in swaddling clothes, and laid him in a manger; because there was no room for them in the inn" (Luke 2:6–7).

"And there were in the same country shepherds abiding in the field, keeping watch over their flock by night. And, lo, the angel of the Lord came upon them, and the glory of the Lord shone round about them: and they were sore afraid. And the angel said unto them, Fear not: for, behold, I bring you good tidings of great joy, which shall be to all people. For unto you is born this day in the city of David a Saviour, which is Christ the Lord. And this shall be a sign unto you; Ye [You] shall find the babe wrapped in swaddling clothes, lying in a manger. And suddenly there was with the angel a multitude of the heavenly host praising God, and saying, Glory to God in the highest, and on earth peace, good will toward men" (Luke 2:8–14).

"And it came to pass, as the angels were gone away from them into heaven, the shepherds said one to another, Let us now go even unto Bethlehem, and see this thing which is come to pass, which the Lord hath made known unto us. And they came with haste, and found Mary, and Joseph, and the babe lying in a manger. And when they had seen it, they made known abroad the saying which was told them concerning this child" (Luke 2:15–17).

I want you to know that this story is true.

TO THE TEACHERS

Well, now that school is underway, and you're probably getting back into your routines, I would like to share a story that I believe is probably more of a legend than a fact, but it makes a powerful point.

It seems that a traveler in the eastern country overtook an old gentleman one day walking toward a town. The traveler asked the old man, "Who's the great man of that little town? Who's your leading man? Who's the governor and controlling spirit of that little place?"

The old gentleman replied, "I am the king of that little town."

"Really!" said the traveler. "Are you the leading man?"

"Yes, Sir. I am king in that place, and I reign as king."

"Well, how do you make this to appear? Are you in affluent circumstances?"

"No, I am poor. But in that little village there are so many children. All those children go to my school. I rule the children, and they rule the parents. And that makes me king."

Well, even though I'm a teacher, I'm also a dad. So, I would like to speak as a father to those "kings" who teach the children—my children:

Teacher, please teach the truth, the pure, unadulterated truth.

Teacher, you are not better than your student, but that student has been taught to trust you.

Teacher, what you are speaks louder than what you teach. Long after your students have forgotten the precepts you taught, they will remember how they felt when they were with you.

Teacher, your students are under attack by destructive forces on all sides. Please, never weaken their armor.

Teacher, this world is full of the unseemly and perverse. May the domain of your classroom be a haven of light and empowering truth.

Teacher, when you enter the heart of that child, you stand on sacred ground. Tread carefully, for surely someday you will be accountable to a greater father than I.

Teacher, the children are hungry. Nourish them with truth and feed them well.

Teacher, my children are mine before they are yours. So, in all that you say and do, please strengthen the bonds of my family. Never—please, never—weaken it.

Teacher, you will have many in your charge, sometimes too many. Please don't forget that your greatest impact will likely be one on one.

Teacher, you hold great influence with your students, and well you should; I hope you do. But remember, you do not need personal disciples.

Teacher, it's a turbulent world out there. I hope your classroom will be a sanctuary where those children are safe.

Teacher, you have the awesome power and ability to open their minds. Open them; open them wide. But when you leave them, may it never be with doubt and error, but always with truth and hope.

Teacher, the world these children are entering is tough, unforgiving, and competitive. Don't coddle them. Stretch them, work them, and teach them to love learning. They will be forever grateful.

Teacher, there is so much of ill manners and crudity in their environment. Please teach them manners and discipline them in the use of those manners.

Teacher, they won't always have you. So, I hope that you will teach them to discover truth on their own and value it. Remember, what you are making of the children is not "a graduate," it's a citizen.

Teacher, please speak plainly. Don't attempt to dazzle them with your brilliant intellect. Teach them in such a way that they cannot possibly misunderstand the truth.

Well, I could go on, but I'll conclude with this:

I know that most of you teachers cannot speak of the God you love in your classroom. But you can speak to God about them—about your students. You can bind them to Him by your prayers and faith, and thereby you can call down His blessings on them. That may be the greatest thing you ever do for them. That may be your greatest demonstration of love.

God bless you noble teachers. We love you; we count on you; may you ever have a burning sense of the trust that has been placed in you by the fathers here and the Father hereafter.

THE LAMB OF GOD

It was Easter Sunday. My family was watching *The Lamb of God* on television, a movie about the life and Atonement of the Savior. I left the room for a moment, and when I returned, I found my eight-year-old daughter curled up on the floor, hiding her eyes and crying.

"It's scary!" she said. "I don't want to watch it."

I looked at the screen. The Savior was stretched out on the ground, and the big Roman hammer had just driven the nails into His hands. I picked her up off the floor and cradled her on my lap. She snuggled in tight, and I explained what was happening and why as we watched Jesus be lifted up on the cross and die. I told her how Jesus suffered as payment for our sins and our mistakes so that we wouldn't have to pay for them if we repent.

The scenes then changed to the morning of the Resurrection. I narrated the movie as Mary came to the tomb and found it empty, and as Peter and John ran to see for themselves. I explained the significance of John standing alone in the empty tomb and turning back to look one more time. He believed!

I really wanted Hannah to understand that, yes, it is a scary movie, but it has the happiest ending of all time.

After the movie was over, I was standing alone in the kitchen wondering if she really did understand. If ever there was a question for the ages, it has to be, *Why was it necessary for Jesus to suffer and die in such a horrible way?* And if ever there was anything absolutely vital to understand, it's the Atonement of Christ.

I called her to me, squatted down on her level, and asked, "Hannah, why did Jesus have to die in such a scary way?"

She looked at me and said, "So that when we make sin, we don't get in so much trouble." The answer was classic.

The Psalmist said, "Out of the mouths of babes . . . thou hast perfected praise?" (Matthew 21:16, in reference to Psalms 8:2). In her simple and profound way, she was absolutely correct! Because of Him, we don't have to get in so much trouble. He paid a scary price indeed for our sins. Why?

My dear friends, please repent. For if you do not, your sins will be paid for twice—once by Him and again by you, and both in the most scary way imaginable!

As for my beautiful daughter, I smiled and gave her a hug. For now, she understands enough.

"Are You John Peter Malmberg?"

John Peter Malmberg joined The Church of Jesus Christ of Latter-day Saints in 1858 when he was thirty-one years old. Because of his Church membership, he was fired from his job as a steel worker. With his talents and tools, John did the best he could to provide for his family, all the while hoping that he could soon emigrate to Utah and join the Saints.

John had been promised by a friend money for travel to America, but that money did not come. Then on January 1, 1863, a Church meeting was held in Stockholm where plans were being made for those emigrating that year. Though he had no means to make the journey, John felt prompted to attend.

John arrived at the meeting and realized he didn't know anyone there. Reportedly, a man walked up to him and asked, "Are you John Peter Malmberg?"

John replied, "I am, but I do not know you. I have never seen you before; how did you know my name?"

The gentleman explained, "I am Anders Eliasson, and you were shown to me in a dream last night. I am supposed to let you have money to take your family to Utah."

Anders Eliasson was a shoemaker and craftsman living on a comfortable estate in Sweden. His wife had become converted, but Anders had not. Then one night in 1861, he experienced a dream where he was told to get up and read a certain passage from the Bible. He did so. A few days later, missionaries stopped by their home. Anders joined the Church shortly thereafter.

Out of the goodness of his heart, Anders helped more than one hundred people, including John Peter Malmberg, emigrate to Zion; the shoemaker helped many walk to Zion. In 1863, Anders and Christine took their family and, after enduring many hardships, came to Utah and settled in Grantsville.

Though many families were given the means to journey to Zion by Anders Eliasson, evidently few paid that money back. One of those who did was John Peter Malmberg.

Sources: https://www.familysearch.org/tree/person/memories/KWJ1-RMN
https://www.familysearch.org/tree/person/memories/KWVS-7LV

THE BATTLE
HAS BEGUN

The mind and heart of God are not the mind and heart of men. What is worthy of remembering in the eyes of God is often trivial and of no consequence to men. In that light, this story is an effort to remember a monumental moment in the eternal affairs of this earth. It is dedicated to those modern warriors of light anxiously engaged in the cause of Christ.

Late one fall evening after Heber and Vilate Kimball had retired to their bed, they were awakened suddenly by a sharp knocking at their door. A neighbor, John Greene, stood at the door and bade them come out and see the incredible scenery in the heavens.

They did so, and it was a beautiful starlit New England night, so exceptionally clear and brilliant that Heber later said he could have seen well enough to pick up a pin.

As the little group watched, a white smoke or cloud formed on the eastern horizon and slowly began to rise upward. As it did so, it formed itself into a belt spreading across the sky toward the southwest, and it was accompanied by the sound of a mighty, rushing wind.

Gradually, the belt flattened out and broadened across into a bow—like a rainbow—becoming transparent with a bluish cast and stretching from horizon to horizon.

No sooner had that bow formed than an army of men appeared arising from the east and began marching twelve abreast across the bow toward the west. As vivid and real as men in the flesh, they marched in the most profound order, every man stepping in the tracks of his leader in perfect synchronization. They were dressed in the full battle gear of nineteenth-century soldiers, including muskets and bayonets. They were so clear and distinct that Heber and the small group of neighbors could distinguish the features of their faces and hear the jingle of their equipage as they moved.

Shortly, the entire bow from horizon to horizon was crowded and filled with marching men, the sound of that marching clearly reaching the ears of the astonished onlookers.

Heber later described the event this way: "No man could judge of my feelings when I beheld that army of men, as plainly as ever I saw armies of men in the flesh; it seemed as though every [the very] hair of my head was alive."

When the celestial army reached the western horizon, they were met by an opposing force, and a battle ensued. The sound of the rush of men and the clash of the arms was distinct and unmistakable. Heber and his friends looked upon this scene for hours until it gradually disappeared.

Heber's wife, somewhat afraid, turned to one of the older men in the group and asked, "Father Young, what does all this mean?"

"Why, it's one of the signs of the coming of the Son of Man," he replied.

And indeed it was, even though the world missed it, just as surely as the meridian world missed the birth of Christ. For you see, that momentous night marked the commencement of the marvelous work and wonder spoken of by Isaiah. That significant night, that night of nights in an eternal sense, was September 22, 1827—the same night that just twenty miles away at a place called Cumorah a young man named Joseph Smith was receiving the plates of the Book of Mormon from an angel named Moroni.

The war in heaven never ended. It just changed battlefields, and once more the battle between good and evil had begun. Welcome to the war!

KATIE'S PRAYER

When we pray and expect a spectacular or grand answer, as we oftentimes do, we miss the way our Heavenly Father most frequently answers our prayers.

For three years, Katie and her family lived in Argentina. At that time, Katie was a tiny, bubbly, eight-year-old the Argentines affectionately referred to as *la petisa*, which means "the petite one."

A necessary part of the family's experience in Argentina was the dreaded gama globulin shot, which they had to receive every three months. When it came Katie's turn for her shot, she said to her mother, "Mother, I just can't do it. It hurts so much."

Mom tried to reason with Katie, explaining to her how vital the shot was for the protection of her health.

"I know, Mommy, I know," Katie said. "I don't want to be sick, but I don't want to get the shot."

Mom looked at her lovingly and said, "It's okay, sweetheart. Why don't you go to bed tonight? I'll put the syringe in the refrigerator, and we'll talk about it again tomorrow."

Katie went to bed, as did Mom and Dad. A short time later as Dad finished his personal prayers, he noticed that his wife was gone.

When she returned, she had a strange look on her face. "You'll never believe what I just did," she said.

"What did you do?"

"As I was praying, I had the impression that I should give Katie her shot while she was asleep. I got up, went downstairs, got everything ready, and went quietly into Katie's bedroom. There she was with her arm exposed outside the sheet, and I thought to myself,

What a witch of a mother I am. I gave Katie the shot and she did not budge. Can you imagine me doing something that terrible?"

The next morning, Mom confessed to Katie, "Katie, you'll never believe what I did last night."

"What, Mommy?" Katie asked with a surprised look.

"Last night, while you were asleep, I gave you your shot."

For a moment Katie looked at her mother in disbelief, and then she began to cry. "Oh, Mommy," she said, "last night I prayed that I could get my shot, but that it wouldn't hurt. Mommy, I didn't even feel it."

Adapted from an experience by Katie Moore as told by her father, Gary Moore.

THE ROCK OF OFFENSE

Not long ago I got really curious and looked up *rock* and *stone* in the topical guide of my scriptures. I learned some interesting things.

First, I learned that Christ was often referred to as the *Rock of Salvation* and *the only sure foundation of righteousness*. That seemed a fitting metaphor—because, like a rock, He's strong, firm, unchanging, and enduring, capable of weathering the storms and bearing our weight.

Second, I noticed that when the Lord and His people entered into covenant relationships, there were usually stones piled or fitted in the form of altars or pillars that served as continual reminders of those covenants. I learned that the covenants should be as enduring and unchanging as the stones themselves.

Given all these qualities about Jehovah, why is it that God's people over the last six thousand years have so frequently fallen into apostasy and been destroyed? I found the answer to that question the hard way—literally!

In an effort one day to teach some young people this principle about Christ being the Rock, I brought in to my classroom a huge square lava rock that probably weighed about two hundred pounds. Using the rock, I explained that because of the nature of this type of stone, its strength, and its durability, it was often used years ago to build foundations for homes. We then discussed how the Savior was like that stone, sure and solid, unchanging, able to be the foundation for our eternal house of faith.

However, I explained, for those who will not trust the Savior and follow Him, He becomes a continual nuisance. He becomes the stone in your path on a dark night that causes you to stumble, or worse yet, the stone that falls on you and crushes you when you least expect it. The Savior is the stone that will not go away and cannot be avoided.

Well, I used that rock throughout the day to make my point. You know, looking back, I think it went well.

Late that night, after teaching an evening class, I turned off the lights and strode quickly toward the exit of my classroom. Yep, you guessed it! Suddenly, something caught both my shins, causing me to stumble and fall headlong to the floor. I had forgotten my rock. I lay there wounded and bleeding in intense pain, wishing I had remembered. It took weeks for my wounds to heal.

Just like ancient Israel, I had forgotten Him who must not be forgotten nor ignored. I hadn't meant to. I just forgot!

The Psalmist once said, "Hear my cry, O God; attend unto my prayer. From the end of the earth will I cry unto thee, when my heart is overwhelmed: lead me to the rock that is higher than I" (Psalms 61:1–2).

MARYANN'S RACE

I have a question: Are the obstacles too much sometimes? Have you ever felt like you just didn't want to try again, and that if you did, you'd just fail anyway? Well, if this sounds familiar, I would like to tell you a story about a young friend of mine.

MaryAnn saw the truck a split second before the impact. Her next recollection was of hearing someone calling her name. Opening her eyes, she looked down and saw her legs grotesquely broken and bowed. The incredible force of the collision with the truck had driven the van's dashboard into the front seats and into her legs, breaking her left leg in a dozen places and snapping the bone in her right thigh.

Rescuers extricated MaryAnn by cutting off her door and her seatbelt. As she was loaded into the ambulance, her legs throbbed with a strange feeling of pressure, and the pain was increasing. Every bump in the road sent spasms of pain through her.

Within minutes, she was at the hospital, where, after extensive X-rays, surgeons installed metal rods that ran from hip to knee in both legs.

The significance of this story: MaryAnn had been an athlete, a competitive swimmer with hopes of one day making it to the Olympics. Against some sixty other swimmers, she won the local swim-a-thon in 1998 with a time of 1 hour, 29 minutes, and 30 seconds. Her next goal had been to win that competition again, this time beating her own time. But now. . . .

With the help of two people and a walker, MaryAnn attempted to stand up the day after the accident, but the pain was so intense she nearly fainted. And thus began one of the greatest challenges of her young life.

The next day, she managed three steps and eighteen inches. The pain was nearly unbearable. After six days in the hospital, she went home. It took three people fifteen minutes just to get her in the car. Again, she felt every bump in the road.

With the daily help of a physical therapist, MaryAnn progressed from walking six feet to ten feet, and then forty. When she finally went back to school, it was in a wheelchair, then with a walker, then on crutches, and then with just one crutch.

One month after the accident, MaryAnn returned to the water—only to discover that the metal rods in her legs threw off her balance. Moreover, she was unable to kick her feet or push off the wall. She would have to learn to swim all over again.

The day of the swim-a-thon approached. Winning was out of the question. But should she at least enter and try to finish it? Could she? Several people warned her not to try, fearing that she would hurt herself. Some even thought she was joking for even considering it. But with a determination as hard as the steel in her crippled legs, MaryAnn resolved to enter the race and at least finish it.

The day of the race, still in therapy, unable to walk or run without a limp, or even jump off the ground, MaryAnn got in the pool to race. Two hundred lengths and some three miles later, the whistle blew. MaryAnn had won. Her time: 1 hour, 29 minutes, 30 seconds—exactly the same time as the year before.

My friends, those of you who have tried and failed, the Master said, "With faith, all things are possible."

I witness that if our personal goals are worthy and important to us, then they are important to Him, and He will help us. But please know this: Our pain and our sacrifices in the obtaining of those goals in the victories we win are as critical to our growth as the victories themselves. Try again.

My Mind Is Mine

Late one evening many years ago, a friend and I were riding bicycles as we returned from an appointment. In order to get where we were going, we had to cross the oncoming lanes of traffic on a busy street. I could see a car coming up ahead, but I had plenty of time. I made the left-hand turn without problem. But my friend was too close to the oncoming car to make the turn. He decided to try it anyway, speeding up and darting in front of the car.

As he was doing these death-defying shenanigans, I was looking back over my shoulder, watching and holding my breath—still pedaling my bike. I thought for a moment he was going to be a hood ornament with a suit and a smile, but he made it.

However, when I looked back around to the front, my bike had drifted up against the curb. Oh no! I knew what was going to happen. With all my willpower I wanted that bike to go back out in the street where it was safe. But in my panic, all I could stare at was the big, ugly curb that was going to get me.

Well, it got me! My bike hit the curb and went out from under me. I flew through the air, landing on my back and sliding in the slimy, wet, green grass. My freshly cleaned suit was a mess, and my pride was worse.

I learned from that experience and others like it that wherever I'm looking, that is where my bike, my car, my body, or my life will go. Please consider—what you see is generally what you think, and what you think is generally what you do. If your mind, heart, ears, and eyes are constantly filled with and focused on the distracting and destructive things of this world, is it any wonder that you are continually crashing? It is a powerful, true principle—applicable in all areas of your life and mine—your mind is yours, and if you make it mind you, your destiny is also yours.

EASTER AND RACHEL

One fall day several years ago while sitting in a Spanish class, a friend of mine, Rachel, was paged to the principal's office. As she entered, she was instructed to go to the home of her grandparents immediately. Feeling confused, she retrieved her books and left. When she got to the house, she went inside and sat down in a rocking chair. Her grandmother sat on the couch nearby. It was obvious she had been crying, but she said nothing. A moment later, Rachel's grandfather walked into the room, placed his hand on her shoulder, and said, "Rachel, your dad was killed in a car accident this morning."

Rachel said, "I felt as if I had been punched in the chest. Breathing was difficult. [I] sat there in shock as the tears rolled down my face and I attempted to make sense of what I had been told. How could he be gone? He would no longer be there to answer my math questions, to take me to scary movies my mom refused to see with him, to take me skiing, to promise me that in high school, boys would realize I was alive, and to take me on daddy-daughter dates. He wouldn't be at my graduation from high school or at my wedding. He wouldn't be there to see me go on my first date." And then she concluded, "The pain of this loss continues to this day."

I became acquainted with Rachel after her father died. One day I could see that she was struggling. So, I invited her and a friend into my office to talk. But she sat there, more or less stone-faced, refusing to say anything. I knew she was hurting, and I had a pretty good idea I knew why. I persisted in trying to get her to open up and share her feelings. Finally, in something of an emotional explosion, she blurted out amidst her tears, "I miss my dad!" and she began to sob.

I'm not ashamed to tell you that those words seared my soul and opened my eyes. I will never forget them. I had no idea what to say to her.

Eventually, Rachel and her family worked through their pain, and they are courageously learning to cope, as have others afflicted with so great a tragedy.

I tell you this tragic, but yet unconcluded story, because nearly two thousand years ago on a hallowed Sunday morning, the Lord Jesus Christ took up His body and left the tomb. He, whose body had been completely destroyed, whose heart had been stilled and broken on the cross of Calvary, came forth from the tomb in glorious, living reality.

But there is more to the story. Matthew records the following: "And the graves [of the saints] were opened; and many bodies of the saints which slept arose, And came out of the graves after His resurrection, and went into the holy city, and appeared unto many" (Matthew 27:52–53).

Rachel's story has not yet concluded because there will come a day when like those ancient Saints, the Savior will come for her father. And her father will come forth from the tomb to live again in the flesh, and his love for her and for his family will have only increased. And that reunion? Well, that's the conclusion of the story. And I assure you, for them and for those who keep the faith, the joy of the future will brilliantly overshadow the pain and losses of the past. This is Easter to me!

Experience of Rachel Harper.

BREAKING A HORSE

Sometimes it doesn't pay to take some things for granted. I learned this lesson a few years ago when I was asked by a friend to break a horse. I was excited. It had been a long time, and I was eager to do it again. I loaded up my family and drove over to see him.

The horse turned out to be a large, three-year-old Appaloosa gelding. I climbed through the fence, and he came right up to me. I was under the impression that he was already mostly trained and that I was only supposed to finish that training. He seemed really gentle, so I saddled and bridled him right there in the pasture and swung up on his back.

When I began trying to neck-rein him and line him out, however, all he did was fight me. But the harder he fought me, the more determined I became that he wasn't going to get away with it. He was going to do things my way, or else. It didn't occur to me at the time that he didn't have a clue what I wanted of him.

Finally, the horse in frustration threw his head in the air and reared up. He went higher and higher until he lost his balance and went completely over backward. It caught me so off guard that I didn't react like I'd been taught; I didn't get away from him in time, and he came right down on top of me. Well, to make a long and embarrassing story short, I was hurt, and it took a long time to get over it.

I found out that the horse wasn't broke at all. He really didn't know anything. Needless to say, from that day on, I handled him much more carefully; I never again took him for granted. And as I learned to respect what he was capable of, I was able to control him and train him to be a decent saddle horse. All in all, it turned out to be a great experience.

Life is a lot like a large horse. If we get overconfident and reckless, and don't treat it carefully and cautiously, it may wind up sitting on our chest, and we will be left lying on the ground spiritually torn, bleeding, and gasping for air. Life can be dangerous; handle it with care, prayer, and Christ.

Oh, and just in case you are wondering, I did get back up, and I did get back on.

REFLECTIONS ON A SKI TRIP

S ometimes the most commonplace of people and events can teach the most profound lessons if you look carefully.

Recently, I took my three oldest children and went cross-country skiing. As our adventure began, the four of us encountered a very steep hill. We're all beginning skiers. While three of us were gingerly inching our way down the hill, my ten-year-old daughter, who seems to have no fear, suddenly came flying past us, digging in her poles to get as much speed as possible. She stayed upright all the way to the bottom of the hill, until her skis went tip first into a drift, and she biffed it right in the drift. She came up laughing; I was laughing too. From the top of the hill I thought, *Why not?* So, I cut loose. I made it all the way to the bottom and landed in a pile right next to her.

Lesson number one: Sometimes in life we are a little too timid. We need to trust the Lord and throw ourselves into life and relationships. So what if we crash once in a while? The fun was worth it.

The weather on our ski trip later turned into a blizzard. I had promised the children when we found the warming cabin at the top of the trail, we'd have hot chocolate and candy for a feast. Getting to the cabin became very difficult, so they began to chant, "Hot chocolate, cabin, candy; hot chocolate, cabin, candy" over and over as loud as they could. We got all the way up to where we thought the cabin should be, and we couldn't find it. I don't think it was there. It was a discouraging moment. We had to turn around and start back without the fire, without the candy, and without the hot chocolate. And there was not one word of whining. What good would it do?

Lesson number two: Sometimes we have to be our own best cheerleader. The world is full of whining, sour-faced, pickle-suckers. We don't have to be one of them. Life is really a lot of fun if you think about it.

We trudged along, falling frequently, until we came to another steep drop-off. At this point, my oldest daughter went off. She made it about ten feet before going face first right into the snow. She came up cold, wet, and sputtering. I heard her mutter as she got up, "I skied up it; I'll ski down it." She got up, she went just a short distance, and down she went again. This time, as she got up, I heard her say, "Well, at least I'm getting good at picking myself up." When she was then upright, she did it again, this time through clenched teeth, saying, "I skied up it; I'll ski down it." She did, too—all the way to the bottom.

Lesson number three: We all need to get good at picking ourselves up. Life certainly has a way of knocking us down—sometimes frequently. And God's way isn't always the easiest way, but it certainly is the most thrilling. Don't take your skis off and don't give up just because the hill gets steep.

Finally, at one point during our trip, my younger daughter took off her skis, and the bindings became iced; she couldn't get them back on. When I came on the scene, I found my son standing in several feet of snow with bare hands and a pocketknife trying to get his sister on her way. He was cold and wet. He could have skied on by and gone right on down the hill, but he didn't.

Lesson number four: I hope he never just goes by. Stopping to help is exactly what his Savior would do.

In conclusion: All things considered, the skiing conditions were lousy that day, but the learning conditions were excellent.

ISAIAH 53

There are certain chapters in the scriptures that are so powerful that to add any commentary seems only to detract from the power and the sweetness of their message. To me, Isaiah 53, which is about the life and the Atonement of Jesus Christ, is one of these kinds of chapters. I'd like to share it with you.

[1] Who hath believed our report? and to whom is the arm of the Lord revealed?

[2] For he shall grow up before him as a tender plant, and as a root out of dry ground: he hath no form nor comeliness; and when we shall see Him, there is no beauty that we should desire him.

[3] He is despised and rejected of men; a man or sorrows, and acquainted with grief: and we hid as it were our faces from him; he was despised, and we esteemed him not.

[4] Surely he hath borne our griefs, and carried our sorrows: yet we did esteem him stricken, smitten of God, and afflicted.

[5] But he was wounded for our transgressions, he was bruised for our iniquities: the chastisement of our peace was upon him; and with his stripes we are healed.

[6] All we like sheep have gone astray; we have turned every one to his own way; and the Lord hath laid on him the iniquity of us all.

[7] He was oppressed, and he was afflicted, yet he opened not his mouth: he is brought as a lamb to the slaughter, and as a sheep before her shearers is dumb, so he openeth not his mouth.

[8] He was taken from prison and from judgment: and who shall declare his generation? for he was cut off out of the land of the living: for the transgression[s] of my people was he stricken.

[9] And he made his grave with the wicked, and with the rich in his death; because he had done no violence, neither was any deceit in His mouth.

[10] Yet it pleased the Lord to bruise him; he hath put him to grief: when thou shalt make his soul an offering for sin, he shall see his seed, he shall prolong his days, and the pleasure of the Lord shall prosper in his hand.

[11] He shall see the travail of his soul, and shall be satisfied: by his knowledge shall my righteous servant justify many; for he shall bear their iniquities.

[12] Therefore will I divide Him a portion with the great, and he shall divide the spoil with the strong; because he hath poured out his soul unto death: and he was numbered with the transgressor[s]; and he bear the sin[s] of many, and made intercession for the transgressors.

My dear friends, I know that Jesus Christ lives and that He is our Savior: He has saved us. Because of Him, though our sins may be as scarlet, indeed they can be as white as snow.

"COME BACK, ELLA, COME BACK"— ELLA JENSEN AND PRESIDENT LORENZO SNOW

At about three o'clock in the morning on March 3, 1891, near Brigham City, Utah, Ella Jensen, nineteen years of age, lay in bed grievously ill with scarlet fever. Suddenly she sat up in bed and announced, "They are coming to get me at ten o'clock this morning." When asked who was coming to get her, Ella proclaimed, "Uncle Hans Jensen and the messengers. I am going to die, and they are coming at ten o'clock to get me and take me away."

Ella insisted on spending the rest of her time in mortality preparing to die. With the help of her nurse, she brushed and fixed her hair. Then she called each of her family members and bid them goodbye. The last one to arrive was her brother, Budd. As he walked in, she "threw her arms around her brother's neck, kissed him, and then fell back on her pillow—dead. It was just ten o'clock."

The family grieved at her loss. Her father, Jacob Jensen, set out for Brigham City, where President Lorenzo Snow was in a meeting at the Tabernacle. Jacob's intent was to ask President Snow if he would speak at Ella's funeral. When Jacob arrived at the Tabernacle, the meeting was in progress.

I went into the vestry, behind the main hall, wrote a note [to President Snow]. When the note was placed on the pulpit, President Snow stopped his talking, read the note, and then explained to the saints that it was a call to visit some people who were in deep sorrow and asked to be excused.

Rudger Clawson, who was serving as president of the Box Elder Stake, was invited by President Snow to go with him to the Jensen home. As they entered, President Snow stood at Ella's bedside for a minute or two, saying nothing. He then asked if there was any consecrated oil in the house. President Clawson described what happened next.

Turning to me President Snow said, "Brother Clawson, will you anoint her?" Which I did. We then laid our hands upon her head and the anointing was confirmed by President Snow, who blessed her and among other things, used this very extraordinary expression, in a commanding tone of voice, "Come back, Ella, come back. Your work upon the earth is not yet completed, come back." Shortly afterward we left the home.

Ella's father recorded what happened next:

Ella remained in this condition for more than an hour after President Snow administrated to her, or more than three hours after she died. We were sitting there watching by the bedside, her mother and myself, when all at once she opened her eyes. She looked about the room, saw us sitting there, but still looked for someone else. And the first thing she said was: "Where is he? Where is he?" We asked, "Who? "Where is who?" "Why, Brother Snow," she replied. "He called me back."

Ella described in great detail what and who she saw in her three-hour sojourn in the spirit world. There was no doubt in anyone's mind the truth and veracity of her story. She told of meeting many people, relatives and friends, and of being in a large hall with many children and Aunt Eliza R. Snow when she heard the voice of President Snow commanding her to come back. Reluctantly, for she hated to leave, she turned around and retraced her steps back to her body. The rest of her story is incredible. Ella lived to be eighty-six years of age and bore eight children.

And as for President Lorenzo Snow, there is one more thing. Under the hands of Patriarch Joseph Smith Sr., Lorenzo Snow was given a patriarchal blessing in the Kirtland Temple in 1837. It said in part:

> "Thou shalt become a mighty man. Thy faith shall increase and grow stronger until it shall become like Peter's. Thou shalt restore the sick; the diseased shall send to thee their aprons and handkerchiefs, and by thy touch their owners shall be made whole. The dead shall arise and come forth at thy bidding."

Sources: http://www.ldsscriptureteachings.org/2016/12/13/ella-jensen-raised-from-the-dead-by-lorenzo-snow/
LeRoy C. Snow, "Raised from the Dead," Improvement Era,: Vol. 22 (September 1929), 881–886, 972–980.

FAITH TO WALK ON WATER

Have you ever felt that your faith was just not enough to handle this stressful world? I have, and that's why this story gives me hope.

Jesus came walking on the Sea of Galilee sometime around 3:00 in the morning in the midst of a terrible storm. The disciples saw Him and cried out in terror, thinking He was a spirit.

Jesus bade them, "Be of good cheer; it is I; be not afraid" (Matthew 14:27).

Still wondering in the darkness if it were really the Master, Peter asked if he might come out to the Savior on the water.

Jesus's answer was an invitation that must have completely stretched Peter. Jesus said simply, "Come" (Matthew 14:29).

And Peter did it; he walked on the water—that is, he did it as long as his gaze was fixed on the Master. But the boisterous waves broke his concentration. Peter looked away from the Savior in fear and immediately began to sink.

"Lord, save me!" he cried out (Matthew 14:30).

The Lord stretched forth His hand, caught Peter, and lifted him back up on the water.

Together they returned to the boat. Amazingly, the winds ceased and there followed a great calm.

Jesus said to Peter, "Oh thou of little faith, wherefore didst thou doubt?" (Matthew 14:31).

Some may think that Peter failed. But did he—really? His effort increased his faith, and with the Master's gentle correction, he would succeed again.

And so it is with us. Our faith may falter for a time, and this stormy world may threaten to drown us, but if we keep our eyes fixed resolutely on Him and continue forward, He will not only save us, but bring a great calm to our heart.

My faith may be small, but with Him, it's all I need.

THE SOIL

Some time ago, in an effort to teach some high school students a difficult principle, I took them for a walk. As we strolled outside, I pointed out the beauties of the earth—the lush green grass; the tall, majestic shade trees; and the delicate, beautiful flowers. To say that they were less than impressed would be an understatement. I think they suspected that I was up to something.

When we were back in the classroom, I asked them what it was that was responsible for all of that beauty and wonder. I got various answers. At that point, I walked over to one of my many potted plants in my classroom, and I took out a handful of soil. I asked them what it was.

I got the predictable answer: "Dirt."

I then explained to them that *dirt* is a dirty word to a soil scientist.

"It's not dirt," I then explained. "It's soil."

I then asked them to consider how important soil is to us. Well, it didn't take very long for them to realize that soil is a very precious commodity, responsible in large measure for life on this planet. Without it, most, if not all, of us wouldn't be here. It is the essence of life itself. Our bodies are made from the very dust of this earth. What do you owe to dirt? More than you think.

With their understanding of soil now deepened, I took my soil, walked over to the nearest student, and dumped it all over her desk, her books, and I think even her—and if I remember right, I scattered some of it around the room too. My students looked at me with a little shock.

After giving them a moment to recover, I then asked, "All right, now what is it?"

Someone said something like, "A mess."

I then explained that soil in its proper place and time is a wonderful, God-given, life-giving, precious gift. But when it's thrown in the middle of their living room—all over them, their family, and their carpet—it's just cheap filth! It doesn't belong there.

My dear friends, so it is with human intimacy. Sexual relations between a man and a woman legally authorized by God are sacred, God-given, and precious. They are the wonderful source of life and unspeakable joy to God's children. But when sex and the sacred are reduced to cheap entertainment and callously thrown into my living room like so much digital dirt, no longer is it sacred. It is out of its place and time; it becomes filth. And any person who claims a right to pass on this evil has no right and has turned love into a lie.

For the sake of life on this planet, don't let them.

HIS BLOOD

From the moment this earth was formed, it was known that man would make mistakes. It was no surprise that all of us would break eternal laws and fall short of heavenly glory. Thus, a loving Father send His first-born Son to this earth with an endowment of power and a mission to save us all.

For centuries, the faithful brought their lambs to the holy place and killed them by shedding their life's blood. The knife in their hands and the blood on the ground were vivid reminders that someday a damned and helpless humanity would shed the lifeblood of the Son of God. His blood bought us like money in a purchase. The ownership of our souls passed from the devil of hell to the deliverer of heaven. We are His, bought with an infinite price. Is it any wonder that we are continually reminded to remember His offering for us? But, oh, how easy it is to neglect and to forget, especially when the image of blood and suffering is not before our eyes. In that light, I'd like to share a story.

Not long ago, I was trying to put a block of wood in my stove when it slipped and smashed my thumb. The nail instantly turned purple and oh, how it hurt! As the day wore on, the pain of my mistake intensified. Pressure built up under the nail until the pain drove me to distraction. Finally, I took a knife and relieved the pressure. Off and on for the next thirty-six hours I tended to the wounded thumb.

Then came Sunday morning. I went to church and more or less forgot about the wounded thumb. The congregation began to sing a familiar hymn. My wife opened the book and handed it to me. I sang about half of the first verse. When I glanced down at the book, I was shocked to see the brilliant red of my blood on the stark white of the page—my thumb was bleeding again. Embarrassed, I quickly tried to clean my blood off the page.

Then suddenly I became aware of the words the congregation was singing: "I tremble to know that for me He was crucified, That for me, a sinner, He suffered, He bled and died" ("I Stand All Amazed," *Hymns*, no. 193). I stopped singing and looked at the blood on the page; the impression in my mind was too vivid for words.

Now I don't know what to make of this experience, but this much I know: The Atonement of Christ really happened.

His blood was shed to save us from a fate worse than death. My blood on that page was only a few drops. By comparison, His blood was a torrent.

My blood was the result of my own foolishness. His blood heals the wounds of my foolishness.

My blood stained the page. His blood washes and cleanses all of our stains.

My blood and pain were only a moment. His blood and pain touched the infinite and the eternal.

By the grace of God, may we never forget the significance of His atoning blood.

THE CLEANSING

Near the end of the Savior's ministry, two events occurred that have been on my mind. If you don't mind, I'd like to share them.

On the last Monday of the Lord's life, He entered the temple in Jerusalem and found in its courts a scene that angered Him. Flocks of cattle and sheep were milling and bawling; moneychangers with their tables exchanged current coinage for temple coinage that pilgrims might pay the temple tax. Haggling vendors hawked their wares in a scene that would remind us of carnivals at fair time. The noise, the stench, and especially the blasphemous desecration of holy ground moved the Lord to indignant anger. With whip and thunderous command, He drove the moneychangers out into the streets where they belonged. No one dared oppose Him, not even the leaders of the Jews whose pockets were being lined by the ill-gotten gain. Why? Because in guilt there is weakness.

Twice the Lord cleansed the temple, once at the beginning of His ministry and again at the end. I've wondered if there's a broader parallel. The Lord "cleaned house" once on this earth with a flood. The second time it will be with fire—and clean it will be. Of that we may be assured.

The second story takes place the following day, Tuesday. While in the precincts of the temple, Jesus prophesied the total destruction of the temple and denounced the leaders of the Jews for their hypocrisy and corruption. Upon leaving the temple, He retired to the solitude of the Mount of Olives. As He sat, probably looking over the city, His disciples came to Him privately and asked Him when the temple would be destroyed—when would the prophesy be fulfilled?— and what would be the signs of His Second Coming. The Savior's answers to those questions constitute Matthew 24, which we call the discourse on "the signs of the times."

My purpose here is not to enumerate those signs, but to look carefully at the emotional aftermath they had on the disciples. He describes to the Twelve such horrible things as "wars and rumors of wars," "the whole earth in commotion," and "men's hearts failing them for fear just before His coming." He speaks of "the love of men" in our day "waxing cold," of "iniquity abounding," of "earthquakes and desolating sicknesses," and of "men killing one another." When He finishes, the Apostles are visibly scared and upset. Jesus calms them by saying, "Be not troubled, for, when all these things come to pass, you may know that the promises which have been made unto you shall be fulfilled" (D&C 45:35).

If the original Twelve Apostles were troubled by those signs of the times, most of which would not even occur in their lifetime, how much more understandable it is that we in whose day they are being fulfilled should be troubled. Yet, there is no need to let either the signs or the flood of wickedness and corruption around us unduly concern us. I assure you, the Good Shepherd is right on schedule, and He has not abandoned the flock just because of a little bad weather and some ravening wolves among us. I quote Him again: "Be not troubled" (Matthew 24:6).

Tooth Fairy

We have been commanded by our Father in Heaven to "ask, and ye shall receive"—to make all our wants and wishes known to Him (John 16:24). Still, there is a need for judgment and for wisdom in how we pray and for what we pray.

Not long ago, I was traveling back from Wyoming when my cell phone rang. I answered it, and it was my wife wondering where I was. As we talked, I could hear one of my younger children in the background saying, "I wanna talk to Daddy. I wanna talk to Daddy."

Finally, my wife said, "Shaina wants to talk to you."

"Guess what, Daddy?" she asked when she came on the phone.

"What?"

"I lost a tooth."

"You did!"

"Yup."

"You mean you've got a hole in your face now.?"

"Yup."

In order to understand this next part of the conversation, you have to understand that the Tooth Fairy has been a frequent, mysterious visitor to our home through the years.

I said to her, "So, how much do you want the Tooth Fairy to give you for that tooth?"

She thought for a second, and then very matter-of-factly she announced, "Fifty dollars!"

"Fifty dollars!" I said, a little shocked.

"Yup," she said flatly, as if to say, "I've made up my mind, Dad, and this is not negotiable."

Then I found out that after losing her tooth that afternoon at the fair, Shaina had announced to her mother, "Mommy, I'm all grown up now. I'm going to kindergarten, I can ride a two-wheeler, and I lost a tooth. I'm big now!"

I tell you that story to illustrate a point: Sometimes I wonder if we get a little big for our britches with our Father in Heaven—maybe just a little thoughtless in our prayers. I wonder if at times we don't take the time to think very carefully about what we're saying, or sometimes we act as though God works on the same premise as the Tooth Fairy or Santa Claus.

My dear friends, the most perfect kind of prayer is inspired prayer. It is the kind of prayer borne of sincere effort, prayer that brings our mind and heart into unison with our Father in Heaven and brings us to ask for nothing more than what He already wants to give us.

SOUTH TETON

When the Savior said, "Be ye therefore perfect," I'm afraid that some of us may have misunderstood, and it is costing us dearly (see Matthew 5:48).

For a long time, I have wanted to stand atop each of those famous peaks in western Wyoming, the Tetons. A couple of years ago, I was privileged to climb the tallest, the Grand, and I don't hesitate to say it was a life-changing experience.

Not too long ago, I discovered that I had a young friend who not only knew the route to the summit of the other peaks but was willing to take me along. I had had the desire, the strength, and the will to climb all along, but I knew better than to go wandering around up there without a guide.

On the appointed day, we set out for the top. By day's end, we would have ascended 6,500 vertical feet and traveled somewhere between 10 and 20 miles.

As we climbed, our guide, Luke, pointed out the trail and moved up and down the line, encouraging and helping each of the members of our party. He insisted periodically that we stop, rest, and drink plenty of water. There was wisdom in this, even though we didn't feel like resting. During those times we not only were able to rest, but we were able to look back at how far we had climbed and marvel at the view below us. It also gave us a chance to laugh, to joke, and to talk with each other. Little did we know at the time, but these were vital times of refreshing. We wouldn't realize exactly how vital they were until later.

By noon we reached the Garnet Canyon saddle between the middle and south peaks. After a quick lunch, we set out on the last leg of the climb and, I might add, the steepest. Dark clouds threatened bad weather, making it necessary that we waste absolutely no time. I watched some in our climbing party push themselves way too hard, and altitude sickness began to overcome them. Headaches, nausea, and fatigue nearly brought them to their knees. Prudently, the whole group slowed and balanced our pace at the optimum, pushing as hard as we could but resting sufficiently that we could keep everyone in the party still climbing.

Our efforts were rewarded. At 2:00 that afternoon we summited the South Teton, happy as can be, satisfied at our accomplishment—and, I might add, more than a little awed at the grandeur that lay before our eyes.

Earlier in the day, it was hard to listen to the guide at the bottom when he said, "Rest and drink." We felt good. We didn't need to stop; we could push on; we were men! Nevertheless, we did obey, and that careful conservation of energy eventually brought all of us to stand on top—and I emphasize *stand*, not *lay*. It made no difference to me who got there first, as long as we all got there—and we did!

Perfection is the highest mountain in our eternity. We'll be there. It not only cannot be climbed without the constant guidance of One who has climbed it before, the Savior, but it is infinitely more than a one-day or even a one-lifetime jaunt. I believe, as Elder L. Edward Brown said, that, "given enough time and enough people who love you, perfection is not only probable, it is inevitable."

But I add, if there is no joy in the journey now, maybe you're pushing it too hard!

THE EASTER STORY

With Easter comes our opportunity to tell the greatest story of hope ever told.

In spite of the midday hour, darkness covers the land of Jerusalem and the hearts of the people. The Lord Jesus hangs in incomprehensible agony on the cross of Calvary. Standing near the cross are His mother and Mary Magdalene, those devoted and beloved women who accompanied Him, their sufferings surely grievous as they helplessly watch Him die. During those awful three hours from noon to 3 p.m. on that Friday afternoon, Jesus is again afflicted with the exacting pain of the Atonement for the sins of mankind. It is horrible! And then, somewhere around 3 p.m., He cries out with a loud voice, "My God, my God, why hast thou forsaken me?" (Matthew 27:46).

The Father has withdrawn, leaving the victory entirely to the Son. The Lord Jesus has now descended to the very depths, the lowest He can go.

Shortly after that, the Savior, knowing that all things were now accomplished, declared, "Father, it is finished, thy will is done" (JST, Matthew 27:50); "into thy hands I commend my spirit" (Luke 23:46). And the Savior gave up the ghost, His spirit passing at that moment into the spirit paradise that He had so recently spoken of to the penitent thief.

Again, it is now late Friday afternoon. Quickly His disciples and friends take His body down from the cross and hastily place it in a borrowed tomb. The Saturday Sabbath begins shortly. For the few remaining hours of Friday, all of Saturday, and until sometime in the predawn hours of Sunday—or, in other words, over three days' time—the Master's body lies in the tomb while His disciples hide and grieve.

Then, the miracle of all miracles: Jesus returns and takes up that broken and destroyed body, bringing it forth in resurrected perfection and glory. And though it certainly was not necessary in order to release Him from the tomb, the angels come and roll back the stone that sealed the tomb.

It is now just before dawn. Mary Magdalene and the other women come down to the garden tomb, bringing spices to finish preparing His body for proper burial, wondering as they go who will roll back the huge stone to give them entrance. But as they approach the tomb in the dim light, not only is the stone already rolled back, but two men whose countenances are as brilliant as lightning are sitting on the stone. They say to the women, "He is not here: for he is risen. . . . Come, and see the place where the Lord lay" (Matthew 28:6). The angels continue, "go quickly, and tell his disciples that he is risen from the dead" (Matthew 28:7).

Mary leaves the tomb, evidently not completely understanding what it means. She runs and tells Peter and John, "They have taken away the Lord out of the sepulcher, and we know not where they have laid him" (John 20:2). Jesus had told them repeatedly that He would rise again the third day. But they don't understand; how could they? Such a thing has never occurred in the history of mankind.

Peter and John leave immediately and run to the tomb—and sure enough, the tomb is empty. They return home, leaving Mary alone at the tomb. Mary stoops down, weeping out of grief and loss, and peers into the darkened tomb. The linen grave clothes lie as they were, the body of Christ having passed through them.

The two angels, evidently not visible to Peter and John, are sitting where the body of Jesus had lain. They speak to her, saying, "Woman, why weepest thou? and She sayeth unto them, Because they have taken away [the body of] my Lord, and I know not where they have laid him" (John 20:13).

At that moment, Mary perceives someone behind her. She turns around. It is, she supposes at a glance, the gardener. He speaks to her, saying, "Woman, why weepest thou? whom seekest thou?" (John 20:15).

Mary supposes again that this is the gardener, and she says to Him, "Sir, if thou hast borne him hence, tell me where thou hast laid him, and I will take him away" (John 20:15).

The man talking to her is Jesus, but she doesn't know that. And then He says only one word to her, but oh, the significance and the familiarity of that word. He says simply, "Mary" (John 20:16).

Instantly, she recognizes Him, and her tears of pain and loss are transformed into those of the most transcendent joy. She runs to Him. "Rabboni," she cries out, meaning, "My beloved Master" (John 20:16). And indeed, He was that to her, and indeed He must be to us.

Mary's world changed forever at that moment, as did ours. Can you imagine the significance of her seeing Him? Everything He had ever taught—everything now had greater authority, greater power, greater believability. He was no longer dead. He was a living person of flesh and bone. And because He was, so will we be. All our eternal possibilities stand or fall on the reality and the truth of His Resurrection. This is the core center of Christianity.

I declare to you, "He lives, and while He lives, I'll sing." Joy, power, peace, priesthood, love, and family do not end with the grave because of Him. "He lives! All glory to His name! He lives, my Savior, still the same. Oh, sweet the joy this sentence gives: 'I know that my Redeemer lives'" ("I Know That My Redeemer Lives," *Hymns*, no. 136).

Adapted from Matthew, Mark, Luke, and John.

PRODIGAL SON

Have you ever noticed in your personal discipleship how hard it is to change? If you've struggled with little habits, imagine how hard it is for someone to change who's been trapped by a lifestyle for a long time. It's hard. I know! I've often been asked, "What's the most effective way to help someone who wants to change?" Maybe the following story will help answer that question.

In the parable of the prodigal son, as the rebellious son came to himself and realized his folly, he determined to go home and beg forgiveness and employment of his father, that he might at least eat decently. He set out for home.

The scripture records—and this is the point—that while "he was yet a great way off, his father saw him, and had compassion, and ran" and threw himself upon the boy's neck (Luke 15:20). The father kissed him, heard his confessions, and, rejoicing, brought him once more into the family circle.

I've wondered: How did that father even know he was coming, unless he'd been watching for him? Anxiously that father had watched and waited, and the moment that boy came into view, the father ran all the way out to meet him, quick to forgive.

I believe that it is the same with our Heavenly Father. He is not sternly aloof, withholding His love until the very last steps of repentance are walked. He doesn't demand of us to take every return step alone. He loves us so compellingly that our first feeble steps in His direction are answered with marathons in return. I believe that no one returns to the fold alone.

When through repentance people return, if our celebrations could be as festive and forgiving as those in heaven, maybe more people would undertake the journey.

Adapted from Luke 15:11–32.

BUT IF NOT

There are three words from the Old Testament that recently have taken on very deep significance for me. They are the words *but if not*.

Anciently, in the province of Babylon, King Nebuchadnezzar set up a ninety-foot golden image and commanded all the people of his kingdom, including the Hebrews, to worship it at the sound of the music. If they did not, they would die in the fiery furnaces that same hour by the king's decree.

The statue was unveiled in all of its splendor, and at the given signal, the people bowed before the idol—all except three faithful Hebrews, Shadrach, Meshach, and Abed-nego. They refused to bow, and of course were accused before the king. They were brought before him, and the king again offered them a chance to comply and bow before the idol. He threatened them again with the fiery furnace if they did not. There was no hesitation in their reply: "our God whom we serve is able to deliver us from the burning fiery furnace, and He will deliver us out of thine hand, O King. But if not, be it known unto thee, O King, that we will not serve thy gods, nor worship the golden image which thou hast set up" (Daniel 3:16–18).

That was not the answer the king wanted to hear. In a rage, he commanded that the furnace be heated seven times hotter than usual, and he had them cast into it. So hot was the furnace that it killed the soldiers who threw them in, but Shadrach, Meshach, and Abed-nego fell into the furnace and were unharmed. They were delivered by the angel of God.

In the example of these three men, there's a lesson in faith that I can understand. They said to the king in essence the following: "We know that God has the power and can deliver us, but whether He will now that we live or die, we don't know. But it makes no difference. No matter how hot that furnace, we will still trust Him and not yield to wickedness. Burn us if you will!"

That inspires me. God bless those mighty heroes among us now—those who submit sweetly to God's will, praying and hoping for miracles of deliverance from life's fiery trials. But if they're not forthcoming, they are still true! Oh, how He loves you.

Adapted from Daniel 3.

GIDEON

For those working hard now on your New Year's resolutions and other goals, may I share a key to success with you? It is found inside the story of Gideon, the mighty warrior of Israel's past.

A people called the Midianites had conquered Israel and destroyed their land, leaving them with little food. The Lord came to a young man, a farm boy named Gideon, and called him to free Israel. Gideon humbly protested the Lord's choice, not feeling worthy, but the Lord made it known to him that he was indeed the man chosen to free Israel.

Gideon subsequently gathered an army of 32,000 men to go to war against the Midianites and drive them out of the land. But the Midianites came into the land with an army of 135,000 men. Now get this: The Lord then spoke to Gideon and told him he had too many men. Yeah, that's right: *too many men!*

The way I figure it, the odds were four to one against Gideon, and the Lord said he had too many men? Obediently, Gideon stepped forward and asked his assembled troops how many of them were afraid to go into battle. At that point, 22,000 men raised their hands, and Gideon sent them home. He was now left with an army of 10,000 to fight an army of 135,000.

That makes the odds approximately thirteen to one. Yet still, the Lord told Gideon he had too many. He then reduced Gideon's army to a measly three hundred men. Now get it: The odds are now four hundred and fifty to one. The Lord told Gideon, "By the three hundred . . . will I save you, and deliver the Midianites into thine hand" (Judges 7:7). Why? The Lord does not waste words or time or effort. There had to be a reason for this. Why did He do this to Gideon?

The story continues: Gideon took his three hundred men and divided them into three companies, giving each man a lantern, a trumpet, and a pitcher. Late that night after the Midianites went to bed, Gideon's men came down off the mountain and surrounded the Midianite camp.

Suddenly, at Gideon's signal, each man broke his pitcher, waved his lantern, blew his trumpet, and shouted, "The sword of the Lord, and of Gideon" (Judges 7:20). And can you imagine the chaos that exploded in the Midianite camp?

The Midianites bailed out of bed in stark terror, grabbing their swords as they ran. While Gideon and his men made all the noise and commotion they could, the Midianites in the darkness and confusion couldn't tell a friend from a foe, and they started running around and killing each other. When it was all over, 135,000 Midianites were driven and dead, and Israel was free.

So grateful were the Lord's people that they offered to make Gideon and his sons kings. But Gideon declined. He did lead Israel, however, in peace and righteousness for the next forty years. Gideon became a legend in Israel.

Now my question: Why did the Lord reduce Gideon's number? Answer: Because it had to be with Gideon as it must be with us. We must know, as Gideon had to know, that our victories in the large and small battles of life are fought and won by the Lord, not us!

My friend, you cannot win alone! Whether it be the small battle of a habit or the major war against the natural man, victory will come to those warriors, and only those warriors, who rely on the Lord of Hosts, the God of battles.

Based on Judges 6–8.

"Daddy, Help!"

"The Devil is the founder of murder, and works of darkness; yea, and he leadeth them by the neck with a flaxen cord, until he bindeth them with his strong cords forever" (2 Nephi 26:22). From a tender, flaxen cord to an unbreakable, strong cord, the devil's intent is to destroy our agency and thereby destroy us. My family recently learned a terrifying lesson about this.

My beautiful daughters, Sherise, Jo, and Annie, wanted to climb the South Peak of the Three Tetons in Wyoming. In preparation, we called ahead, talked to the rangers, and got ready.

On the day of the hike, we left in good time and started up the mountain. Other than a little altitude queasiness, we did okay. On the way up, we encountered snow fields we were not expecting. I'd been up there several times before and had never seen this much snow that late in the season. We managed to skirt most of them and kept going.

Then we came to one snowfield just below the lower saddle. It was long, wide, and steep. We could not go around it. There was a good trail with deep footholds, so we decided to proceed.

We made it to the Lower Saddle, and all was well. It was a glorious view, and we did the Instagram thing. We decided not to try to make the summit of the South Teton. The weather was threatening, and it was getting late. We started back down and came to that same long snowfield. The alternate route I had planned around it turned out to be untenable. We had to come down the way we went up, but now the snow was softer and the trail more dangerous. We did not have the proper equipment. We were told we didn't need it, but now we *did* need it, and we had no choice but to go on.

I started out ahead, cutting footholds; my daughters came behind me. I was praying continually when suddenly the thought came to me, *Sit down and slide*. I looked down the slope. It was probably more than three hundred feet down and a greater than 45 percent slope with boulders at the bottom. In short, it was dangerous. I hesitated a moment, and the thought came again. So, I sat down and let go.

I picked up speed so fast that for a moment I wondered what I had done. Desperately, I dug my hands and heels into the snow as far as I could, throwing snow like a plow, but still I picked up speed. It felt as though every bit of skin on my hands was being shredded. I was on a course of imminent injury. Then, just before the boulders, the snow softened even more, and I plunged my hands and heels deeper. Somehow it slowed me without flipping me over. I still hit the bottom hard enough to kiss the rocks, but not seriously.

I stood for a moment, trying to shake the pain out of my hands, when I suddenly heard a cry, "Daddy, help!" I looked up in time to see my oldest daughter, Sherise, completely out of control and barreling down the slope. I took off running but knew I wasn't going to make it. She plowed through some rocks sticking up in the snow and then a split second later hit dry ground, folding up like a pocketknife and going head-first into the boulders.

For a moment she did not move. Then she slowly began to come to. There was no way to know how badly she was injured, but it was clear she was hurt. After a few minutes, she asked me for a blessing. Right there on the mountain, I blessed her to be well and to be attended by angels. A few minutes later she stood up, and, moving slowly, made her way off the mountain. She was bruised more deeply than I have ever seen, but by some miracle nothing was broken, and she sustained no permanent damage.

She later told me what happened. She was the last in the

procession on the snowfield. She watched me slide down and knew she was not going to try that. She stepped forward with her right foot and as her weight came down on it, it slid out from under her—slowly at first. She thought, "I've got this," but when she tried to pull it back, the left foot gave way. In a moment she was out of control and all she could think of was to scream, "Daddy, help!" I still hear her voice in my head. I don't think I will ever forget it.

How much like life is Sherise's experience. Some of us in life venture into places we should not go. We think we can handle it. We step out onto slippery slopes and before we even know what is happening, we are sliding out of control.

It would be trite and cruel to say we should never step into such dangerous territory, but we do—we all do! I can't tell you how many times I've found myself where I shouldn't be, and injury always followed. But somehow, I learned that in such moments I should cry, "Daddy, help!" I have, and my Heavenly Father has always met me at the bottom, blessed me, and gotten me back on my feet.

Source: Family experience, July 2020, Teton Range, Wyoming.

Band-Aids and
Sunsets

On a recent autumn morning, I stood transfixed, and watched the first glorious rays of the sun break the horizon. Oh, it was beautiful! I felt a surge of joy. It was invigorating. That night at 6:56 p.m. from a commanding overlook, I watched that same blazing sun sink below the horizon. It was a strange mix of feelings. As its last rays disappeared, I felt a strange sense of loss, almost a feeling of panic, especially as I turned and looked over the city below me. The brilliant colors that were there a moment ago were gone. The whole city was bathed in darkness and gloom.

Ours is a world of stark contrasts. The earth in its natural state is a thing of beauty; it was created by God. It bears glorious witness of its creator. Yet, for all its beauty, the sun is setting on the society that inhabits it. Our civilization plunges deeper and deeper into darkness, gloom, and filth. What do we do? What can we do? Well, I don't have all the answers, but maybe in this story there is a partial answer.

Not long ago, I overheard a conversation between members of my family and a friend. They were complaining about the ills and evils of certain television programs. I stood and listened. After some time, they dispersed, and I walked into the room.

One of my daughters looked at me and said, "Oh, Dad, my stomach hurts."

At that moment, a bizarre idea struck me. Dad is always a teacher. "I know just what to do," I said, and I ran upstairs.

When I returned, I asked her to show me exactly where it hurt. And she did. I pulled a Band-Aid out of my pocket and I stuck it on her tummy. She gave me the strangest look.

"There," I said with triumph, "doesn't that feel better?"

"No," she said, laughing.

"It doesn't?" I asked, playing stupid. "Well, then I know just what'll fix it for sure."

She laughed even harder when I bent over and kissed her tummy boo-boo.

I looked up at her to see if she understood what I was doing. Not surprisingly, she was completely clueless. She had no idea what I was doing. So I reminded her of the recent gripe session about the television programs.

It took a few minutes, but she came to see that griping and whining about the world's problems are just about as effective as a Band-Aid on a bellyache.

"Don't gripe!" I said. "Do something!"

There are too many in this world today who just want to kiss society's boo-boos and hope they'll go away. They won't! Hasn't history taught us anything?

Here's my point: Those with the power of truth must be doctors to a sick and dying world, or else they will be responsible for the death of it. Come, come all ye sons and daughters of God who bear the covenant of Abraham. The sun is nigh to setting.

COURAGE TO DO RIGHT

S ome time ago, one of my daughters ran into a difficult situation with some friends who wanted to watch a movie with a questionable rating. When asked her opinion, she said she didn't want to watch it. It turned out that she was the only one who didn't, and you can probably guess what happened next. The others began to pressure her, saying things like, "You haven't even seen it. How can you judge it?" Some of them even got mad at her.

Their reaction made her feel bad. It made her wonder if she had done the right thing. Should she have spoken up, or should she simply have been quiet for the sake of peace?

A few days after she told me what happened, I was reading in the scriptures, and a story about the Savior took on a whole new meaning.

One Sabbath Day, Jesus went into the synagogue to teach, and as always, some of His enemies were there. Sitting in that meeting was a man who had a crippled hand. The Savior's enemies watched Him carefully, just to see if He would heal that man on the Sabbath Day, which they considered a great sin.

The Savior knew what they were thinking. He knew that if He healed that man, they'd be offended and there would be trouble.

Look at this situation: Jesus could have ignored the man with the withered hand. He didn't have to help him. He didn't have to say anything. No one would have thought any less of Him if He had simply finished His teaching and gone on His way. After all, He didn't heal every afflicted person He encountered.

But the Savior had more courage than that. He had the courage to do the right thing, even if it would make others angry.

He said to the man with the withered hand, "Stand forth" (Mark 3:3).

The man stood up. Jesus then faced His enemies and asked them if it was wrong to do good. And then He stood there looking at them as He waited for their answer. They refused to answer; what could they say?

Jesus turned to the afflicted man. "Stretch forth thine hand" (Mark 3:5).

As the man stretched out his hand, it was instantly healed and made whole.

The Savior's enemies were so angry, they got up and stomped out of the meeting. That alone would have been bad enough, but they also began putting together a plan to kill Him. The Savior had to leave the area just to stay alive.

Doing the right thing to show off is self-righteous, and that is very wrong. But doing right when you could get away with doing wrong, even if it does offend people, is what it means to be righteous, and that will always take great courage.

Based on Mark 3:1–7.

LOVE ONE ANOTHER

On the very night that Jesus would be delivered up to cruel men to be spit on, beaten, whipped, tortured, and finally killed, the Savior made a crowning pronouncement to His disciples. Knowing full well His fate, He said, "By this shall all men know that ye are my disciples, if ye have love one to another" (John 13:35).

Jesus called it a "new commandment," and well it was. Love was to be re-enthroned once more among the Jews to its rightful place—not as a garnishment to the gospel, but as an essential, driving force in the kingdom of God. The love that the Master intended was to be much more than something we said, much more than an affectionate feeling; it was to be the kind of love that this simple story illustrates.

Grandpa had a date with his four-year-old grandson. They were going to go out for the evening, just the two of them, to a local Salt Lake dance festival.

All was well for a time, but after two hours the little boy got tired of just sitting there. All that music and dancing just wasn't very interesting to him. He began to squirm and to wiggle, and he wanted to wander off. Grandpa didn't want that, so he tried to hold on to the little guy. This only made things more difficult. The little guy began to scream and holler.

Suddenly, without any warning, the toddler doubled up his fist and smacked his grandfather right in the side of the head.

"Grandfather," he shouted, "don't shove me!"

Well, that really rang Grandpa's chimes—woke him right up. His first impulse, he said, was "that the little rascal ought to be spanked."

But then he remembered something that he had seen the little boy's mother do. Rather than give the little guy what some would deem he deserved, Grandpa reached out and gathered him into a tender embrace and loved him. In only a moment the little boy quieted and softened. His chubby little arms reached up and went around Grandpa's neck in complete surrender.

Is this hard? Of course it is! It's easy to say, but it is just exactly as hard to do as it is effective. Think about it: Returning meanness for meanness only yields more meanness. The world was changed once by love, one soul at a time. Why can't it be done again?

As Grandpa said it—Grandpa Harold B. Lee—"If you want to save, that's the method."

Source: Harold B. Lee, The Teachings of Harold B. Lee, *Clyde J. Williams, ed. [Salt Lake City, Utah: Bookcraft, 1996].*

SUMMER THUNDER

One summer while in Salt Lake City for some meetings, my wife and I decided to go to Temple Square to look around. As we drove, I noticed off to the west a big thunderstorm coming in. We arrived just before it hit.

I love thunderstorms. I love to watch them, especially the lightning. Well, when I got there, I wanted to watch that lightning, but I didn't want to get soaked in the process. Then I got an idea. I ran all the way across Temple Square to the North Visitors' Center and up to the second-floor rotunda—the one that has all the windows.

I got there just as the storm hit—and it was a storm! The trees whipped violently in the wind. The rain came down in sheets. It was genuinely funny watching people running for cover. But the most captivating thing of all was the lightning. It wasn't intermittent. It was almost continuous, and it was close! It even knocked out the power to part of the city. I became thoroughly engrossed in the storm.

All of a sudden, I was startled by a voice from behind and above me.

It said, "Learn of me; listen to my words; walk in the meekness of my spirit, and you shall have peace in me."

The timing and effect of those words coming over the sound system was powerful. I became cognizant of where I was. I turned around and found myself standing directly in front of the *Christus* statue. It was a very unique situation.

Outside, beyond those windows, it was a dark, violent, frightening world. But inside where I was, I felt only safety, peace, and calmness. I had no fear of the lightning. I stepped closer to the statue, right between His outstretched arms, and looked up into His face.

For some reason, my eyes were drawn to the prints of the nails in His hands and His feet and the spear mark in His side.

I can't tell you what I felt. I don't know how. But I can tell you this:

I am convinced there is nothing I will ever be able to do to even remotely repay or deserve what He has so freely given. I may be stuck for now in a thunderstorm world, but I don't have to live running around scared. If I come to the Savior, I will always find peace and security in His shelter and joy in the arms of His love.

From an experience in June 1997.

NAAMAN'S MIRACLE

Question: Why should I read the scriptures if the book is boring? Why should I pray? Nothing ever happens. Why should I go to church if I don't get anything out of it? And why should I serve if no one cares whether I do?

I don't think I have a perfect answer, but in the Old Testament there's a story about a man named Naaman, a Syrian. I think there's an answer in this story.

Naaman was a Gentile, not a Jew. He was not a worshipper of Jehovah. He was a pagan idol-worshipper. As a leader of Syria's army, Naaman had delivered his nation out of the hands of the Assyrians. He was considered a great and a good man.

But, Naaman was a leper. And in that day and time, leprosy was called "the living death." There was no known cure—that is, until one day when a little Israelite girl in Naaman's house who served Naaman's wife made the following comment: "Would God my Lord were with the prophet that is in Samaria! For he would recover him of his leprosy" (2 Kings 5:3).

Naaman heard about this. With a glimmering shred of last hope and a small fortune, Naaman set out for Israel, the prophet, and a cure. Riding in the horse-drawn chariot that symbolized his power and position, Naaman came to the door of Elisha's house. From within, the prophet sent a messenger out to Naaman, telling him to dip himself seven times in the Jordan River.

Indignant and outraged that the prophet wouldn't even so much as come out to meet him, Naaman turned away and started for home in a huff. Well, it just so happened that the way home took him relatively near the Jordan River.

As he passed near the Jordan, one of Naaman's servants approached him and said with respect, "My father, if the prophet had bid thee do some great thing, wouldest thou not have done it? how much rather then, when he saith to thee, Wash and be clean?" (2 Kings 5:13).

The way I read that is, "Come on, man, all you have to do is wash. What do you have to lose?"

This was an eternally critical moment for Naaman. Had he shrugged off the counsel of his servant and ignored the prophet, there would likely have been no miracle on Naaman's behalf, and we would not know of the man today. But Naaman made a decision.

He stepped into the water and lowered not only his body, but his haughty pride as well. Seven times he dipped his body into that filthy water. As he rose the seventh time, the scripture records, "He was clean." The leprosy was gone.

Now as then, the Lord's messengers ask us to do some things that make us look pretty silly in the eyes of the world, all the while extending marvelous promises to us and to our families if we will be obedient.

I have a question for you: Did Naaman's leprosy vanish on the first washing? The second? The third? The sixth? No, it vanished the seventh time.

My dear friends, I wonder if we realize that our greatest test in this life is probably not going to be the great challenge that comes only once. Rather, our greatest test in this life is probably going to be the little side journeys of time and obedience—like going to church, reading the scriptures daily, and praying daily—that in and of themselves may seem inconsequential. Yet eventually they will add up to seven, and a miracle!

Based on 2 Kings 5.

JED'S PRAYER

The Lord says in the scriptures, "ask, and ye shall receive" (John 16:24).

I suppose most of us have figured out how to ask, but I wonder how many of us have figured out how to recognize the answer. Our Father can answer His children any way He chooses, but by relating this story, I illustrate how He answers us most frequently.

Not long ago, my wife, Debbie, was helping a friend with a project at the meetinghouse. They found that they needed a hot-glue gun, which my wife had at home. Not having her car, Debbie borrowed Mindy's car and took off for home. As she pulled up in front of the house, she left the car running, thinking that since she knew exactly where the glue gun was, she would be only a moment. With the car running, she closed the door and ran in the house, not realizing that as she did so, the car's doors automatically locked.

When she came back out, of course, she couldn't get into the car. She looked at the coded keypad on the door and thought there was no way she'd be able to guess the right numbers, so she didn't even try. She went back in and tried to reach Mindy by phone, but no one answered.

So, in desperation, she turned to Jed, our teenage son, and asked him to get on his bike, ride up to the meetinghouse, and get the door's number code.

Jed stepped outside. It was 2:30 in the afternoon, and it was hot! There was no way that Jed wanted to pedal two miles just for some numbers.

Jed offered a prayer to Heavenly Father asking Him for help. No sooner had the "amen" been said than a series of numbers came into Jed's mind. He stepped up to the door and punched in those numbers on the five-button, ten-digit keypad. Then he tried the door. It opened!

If we expect the blatant and spectacular to answer our prayers, we likely will not be attuned to that quiet little voice that stirs thoughts in our minds and feelings in our hearts. So subtle are these thoughts that we often pass them by, thinking that they come from us—from within our own minds—and not from God. But, if we will learn to look inward and listen to the thoughts in our minds and the feelings in our hearts, a whole new world will open up. It's called the "spirit of revelation."

MOTHERING UP

When I was a boy growing up on the ranch, we had an annual ritual of the cattle drive, where we drove the herd to the summer pastures in the spring and back home in the fall. It was an exciting time for me, so much so that I never minded always being the one appointed to bring up the rear and eat dust. I remember one drive in particular where we didn't reach the home pastures until after dark. Tired and ready for a rest, I turned my horse toward the barn, but my dad asked me to stay behind and watch the herd.

"Why?" I protested. "They're in the pasture. They're not going anywhere."

He explained that the mother cows and their calves had become separated during the drive. By instinct, he said, the mothers would return to the last place they had seen their calves in an effort to *mother-up*, as he called it. It would be necsary for me to stay behind, ride the fence, and keep all of them in the pasture until all the cows found their calves. It didn't matter if I agreed to stay; I was staying. It was too important.

I had no idea what an experience that would be. I thought the herd would settle right down and all would be well. I couldn't have been more wrong.

It seemed to me at the time as though every critter in that herd was trying to push its way through that fence and go back up the trail. I remember to this day running my horse back and forth in the dark, along that fence, trying to keep those cows and calves in. So determined were they to get out that if they found even the smallest hole, they would stick their head in it and plow right on through. It was a long and frightening night, and I was glad when it was over.

Years later, I began to see a great lesson in that experience. Nature placed a familial bond between those cows and calves so strong that they would fight their way through any obstacle to find each other. Is it all that different with us? We are the children of God. He is our Father—literally. He is part of us, and we of Him. And He has planted within each of us a homing instinct—a drive, if you will—to find Him and our heavenly home. There are times when we sense His presence and yearn for the joy, peace, and love we once enjoyed with Him. And yes, He is calling to us. The question is, will we respond to that subtle instinct within or ignore it?

Will we fight our way through every obstacle and breach every fence in our path to get to Him?

It is my conviction that if we will, there will come a day when we will see His face and hear His voice, and it will startle us just how familiar He is.

THE STORMS OF LIFE

James, the Lord's brother, once said, "count it all joy when ye fall into many afflictions" (JST, James 1:2). Joy? *Joy?* Where is the joy, pray tell, in life's storms? What eternal purpose is served by fear, pain, and struggle? There's an answer to that, and maybe these two back-to-back stories will help us understand.

Years ago, a young friend of mine, a former student, was climbing in the Teton Mountain range. She and her sisters weren't far from the top of Table Mountain when they noticed a big, black thunderstorm coming up behind them.

If you know anything about those mountains, you know that lightning storms in the Tetons are deadly. Stories and legends of killer storms are familiar to anyone who's spent much time there.

As the storm bore down on my friend Sky and her sisters, Sky became anxious and frightened. Should she and her sisters go on to the top and take their chances with the lightning, or should they turn back and get down to lower, safer ground?

Think about it: They had come all this way; they were so close to the summit, but that summit would be the most dangerous in such a storm. This was more than just a fear of getting wet. People have died in these mountains from just such storms.

Now stop for a moment. Why did that storm have to come in the first place? Couldn't an all-powerful, all-knowing God have turned it away? Of course He could. Then answer me this: Why didn't He? And the larger question: Why does He allow Satan to oppose everything we are and everything we do? What I'm really asking is, why does life have to be so hard sometimes? The answer may be found in another story.

A man who was deaf and had a speech impediment was once brought to Jesus. Jesus took the man aside from the group and put His fingers into the man's ears. He then spit and touched the saliva to the man's tongue. Then the Savior sighed, looked up to heaven, and said, "Be opened" (Mark 7:34). The man was immediately healed.

Why did He put His fingers in the man's ears, and why did He put His saliva on the man's tongue? The man was deaf. In a sense, his ears were plugged. By putting His fingers in the man's ears, Jesus communicated His intent to remove the obstruction so that the man could hear. It was a form of communication. And why did He put saliva on the man's tongue? Well, then and now, saliva symbolizes healing. Touching saliva to the man's tongue communicated the message that Jesus wanted to heal his speech impediment.

Why did Jesus do these unusual things—things that some might even consider disgusting? The answer is this: If there is no faith, Jesus can do no miracle. Within that man, the sleeping giant of faith had to be awakened before the miracle could happen. It's no different now. God will do whatever it takes to awaken faith in us, even if that means trials, afflictions, fear, and even thunderstorms when we least expect or want them.

Let's go back to the mountain. As the storm closed in on the girls, Sky and her sisters huddled together, got down on their knees, and asked their Father in Heaven to turn the storm away. Their awakened faith was answered as they stood and watched that mighty storm split, going around them on all sides. Rain fell and lightning flashed all around them, but where they stood it was dry and it was safe. They continued on to the top, and later from the summit of Table Mountain, they watched that storm come back together in all of its fury and lash the peaks of the three Tetons.

That storm became one of the most spiritual experiences in my young friend's life. It can be the same with us and the storms we face. I realize this is hard to say, but don't curse those storms in life, whatever they are and however they come. Use them. Turn in faith and prayer to God, the God whose love never fails, and let Him awaken the sleeping divine giant within you.

Let's thank God for One who loves you just as you are but will never leave you there.

An experience of Sky Gneiting; scripture story adapted from Mark 7:32–37.

THE POWER OF
HIS NAME

A name is an interesting thing; it's more than just a word. A name is a symbol of the person who bears it. The more acquainted I become with you, the more the seeing or hearing of your name will affect me. With that in mind, there is one name we frequently hear and speak as Christians that is more important than any other on earth.

After the Savior's Resurrection and Ascension into heaven, Peter and John were one day entering the temple. It was around three O' clock in the afternoon. As they passed through the gate called "Beautiful," they saw a man who had been lame from birth begging for a handout.

Peter stopped and said to the man, "Look on us" (Acts 3:4).

The man looked at them, expecting to receive something. And I dare say that he was not expecting what he got.

Peter then said, "Silver and gold have I none; but such as I have give I thee: In the name of Jesus Christ of Nazareth rise up and walk" (Acts 3:6).

Peter took the man by the hand "and lifted him up" (Acts 3:7). Immediately the man's legs received strength, and he stood for the first time in his life. As far as I know, Peter performed no corrective surgery, nor did he apply any kind of a brace to help that man stand. He simply spoke a name in faith, and a power was unleashed and set in motion that flowed into the body of that man and healed him. Obviously, that is no ordinary name.

When word got out about what Peter had done, he was questioned by the Jews.

"By what power, or by what name, have ye done this?" they asked (Acts 4:7).

Boldly, Peter declared, "by the name of Jesus Christ of Nazareth . . . doth this man stand here before you whole?" (Acts 4:10). Peter then added this vital truth: "there is none other name under heaven given among men, whereby we must be saved" (Acts 4:12).

I wonder sometimes if we use that name as though it were nothing more than a way to end a talk or close a prayer. I hope not. I hope we understand that that sacred name represents and unlocks the power and authority of God unto our happiness and salvation. All the power of the Atonement is embodied within that name. No wonder we are commanded to be careful how we use it. May we so be.

Adapted from Acts 3–4.

I Love You

"Come unto me all ye that labor and are heavy laden, and I will give you rest" (Matthew 11:28). Those words are true.

Not long ago, someone I know had a simple yet profound experience that I would like to share.

Like many of you, he has many responsibilities that vary from urgencies to emergencies, depending on the day. It's all he can do most times just to keep up, let alone get it all done well.

On this one particular day, he began his morning sometime around 5:30 a.m., and he ran frantically all day long fulfilling various responsibilities. That night as he knelt in a private place to pray, he poured out his heart to his Father in Heaven, expressing thanks and seeking strength. The prayer was not unusual. It was typical of so many thousands he had offered before. However, as he closed that prayer in the name of the Savior and said "amen," in that split second before he could rise to his feet, a voice as clear and distinct as mine came into his mind.

It said simply, "I love you."

The most compelling feeling of love accompanied that voice. Not only did he hear the words in his mind, but a feeling of love and warmth and comfort, something like a heavenly hug, filled his soul. Tears came to eyes that seldom cry. For a few minutes, he remained on his knees basking in the heavenly embrace, letting it wash over and through him. When he finally arose, the burden was gone. His entire outlook was changed. Peace and happiness and confidence replaced the exhausted despair that had been there only a few minutes before. He could do it. Once again, he could go on and face another day. The burden no longer seemed so heavy.

My dear friends, maybe it's trite to say, but it really is true—I know it is. God is there, and He hears us and answers our prayers. He loves us. It is not only possible but inevitable that He will help us carry our burdens, even the mundane ones, if we will work as if it all depends on us and pray as if it all depends on Him.

"FATHER, LET US GO ON"

M oses and Cornelia Clawson were well-established in Steuben County, New York, when in the fall of 1830 they were visited by a Colonel John Stevens who told them a story about a golden Bible. Of that news, Moses later said it "thrilled through me like an electric shock. . . . My desire was to get the book."

He was later able to get a copy of the Book of Mormon, which he read and believed, but there was no one there to teach them more. In 1835, Elders John Gould and Amos Babcock finally taught and baptized the family. As he was confirmed, Moses "was visited with a feeling for several days as though my whole frame was on fire, through which I received great knowledge as pertaining to the things of God."

After baptism, the Clawsons decided to go with others in the area who had joined the Church and gather with the Saints to Missouri by way of Kirtland. On May 11, 1836, they set out. "On the second day of the trip, near the bank of the Genesee River in New York, their 12-year-old son Ebenezer, who was driving the team, was thrown from the wagon. The wagon wheel ran over his body and across his head, cutting his scalp several inches on the back of his head. He seemed dead but came to and said, 'Oh my back.' Moses took Ebenezer down the river one-half mile, where they were furnished a room. News soon spread, and the hotel 'filled with people to see the Mormon boy supposed to be killed.' They were advised to send for a doctor, but none were available. . . . Then four LDS missionaries came in, including Elder Rufus Fisher and an Elder Moon. Moses told them, 'We [are] in [your] hands; now do as you think best.' The leading elder allowed those who wished to remain in the room to stay and then closed the door. Ebenezer was anointed with oil and blessed. The elders told them that in a few hours they could resume their journey. Moses wrote, 'After a time my son awoke and said, "Father, let us go on." We traveled six miles further and camped for the night, my injured son driving the team part of the time. The wound on his head healed without ever swelling, only leaving a scar. We then continued on to Kirtland, where we arrived on the 23rd of May.'"

Source: https://www.familysearch.org/tree/person/memories/KWJX-K5M

THE SKUNK

Many years ago when I was a just boy growing up on the ranch, a friend and I came upon a skunk caught in a trap. That little critter was so hopelessly tangled in the fence that he couldn't move an inch, at least so I thought. I won't bother to tell the whole story here, but I decided I was going to let that skunk go. I had done this before, and I knew that if I was careful, I could do it again. Call me a fool if you want to, but carefully and ever so slowly, I crept toward that skunk. His angry, beady little eyes never left me. I got down within inches of him, and I knelt down to release him.

My fingers were just closing around the trap when my friend spoke loudly and abruptly from behind me, saying, "Hey, you're never going to get him out of there!"

To say the least, he startled me. But what's worse, he startled the skunk! That little beast whirled and sprayed me, hitting me squarely in the face and the chest. I fell back spitting, gagging, and choking! I still remember that taste!

From there, the rest is kind of a blur. I remember heading for home as fast as I could and stripping off my coat and my clothes all the way across the lawn and into the house. I ran straight for the shower. I scrubbed and I scrubbed until the hot water ran out, and then I scrubbed some more. I came out of that shower as rosy and pink as the sunburned nose of a child. When I got through, I couldn't smell a thing. I thought I'd done it.

Then one day not long after that, I was at school playing some basketball with friends. We were playing hard and sweating pretty heavy. Suddenly, one of my friends said, "Oh, you smell that? It smells like a skunk!"

Everyone looked around, but there was no skunk in the room—that is, except this redheaded one. His spray had gotten in my hair, and for months after that whenever I got hot and sweaty, I smelled like a skunk.

I'm here to tell you that that experience and others taught me one of the most fundamental lessons of mortal life: When you keep company with skunks, you stink!

That's not the end of the story. What are you keeping company with? Are you surrounding yourself with influences that stink? The music we listen to, the books we read, and the stuff we bring into our world will either make us happy or will leave us with the depressing stench of a fallen world. Remember, you can no more be happy surrounded by filth than you can smell like roses when playing with skunks!

POWER

Power has always intrigued me, but even the most awesome displays of man's power are puny in comparison to the power of God.

During the Savior's ministry, He was once accosted by a man possessed by a legion of devils. The afflicted man was widely known in the area as a crazy and wild man. He lived naked in the mountains and tombs continually crying and cutting himself with stones. Any previous attempts to restrain and tame him had been answered with his super-human strength. As he broke the chains and escaped, he was more of an animal than a man.

Now, in the presence of the Savior, the possessed man falls at the Savior's feet and worships Him.

At the Master's rebuke, the many devils possessing the man's body request permission to enter the bodies of a herd of pigs feeding on the mountains nearby. The Savior grants it, whereupon the swine run off the cliff into the sea and drown themselves.

When the townspeople come out to investigate, they discover the wild man sitting, clothed and in his right mind. They are sufficiently shocked and afraid at the dramatic events that they send Jesus away without hearing a word.

As to the man, he asked to accompany the Savior, but is instead sent back to his family rejoicing. The Master and His disciples immediately depart.

It appears that the Master's sole purpose that day in crossing the Sea of Galilee was to rescue one soul beyond mortal help. By the power of His word, He cleansed and brought life to the man's soul. And by the touch of His hand, He healed and gave life to the man's body. By the man's faith it was so then, and it is no different now.

THAT ONE YEAR

You know, it's a true principle that God will not do anything to us or for us that is not calculated to benefit us, sometimes even if it has to hurt. The trials of life are at times His way of getting our attention, of humbling us so that He can teach us. If you will forgive a very personal experience, I want to illustrate how I learned this.

There was a period of time in my life years ago when I stubbornly refused to listen to that tiny voice of truth deep in my heart. There was something I knew the Lord wanted me to do, but I refused to admit it. I was the master of rationalizing. As I reflect on it, I think I even had myself convinced.

Then began a year of my life I will never forget. It started when I went out with some friends to do some sleigh riding behind a team of horses. Eagerly I jumped onto the sleigh. But when my friend goosed the horses, they began jumping and jerking back and forth instead of pulling together. As a result, I was pitched forward off of the sleigh and under the horses, and I was bruised up pretty badly. I was sore for a long time.

Shortly after that, I was on my way to take a college final one morning. I was riding a bicycle when a lady ran a stop sign and hit me. I flew high into the air and landed on my head. After an ambulance ride, the worst headache of my entire life, and several hours with a plastic surgeon, my face was sewn together and I was released to heal.

Not too long after that, I sliced open my right thumb clear to the bone at work—another trip to the hospital and more stitches. By now I was getting on a first-name basis with the doctor. He took one look at me and said, "Okay, what did you do now?"

On the day that I got the stitches removed from my right hand, I was told to mount some truck tires—big ones on split rims. I had heard stories about these huge tires blowing apart and killing people. I didn't want that to happen. So, I took what I thought were necessary precautions, which in the end only created a bigger problem. With more than eighty pounds of pressure inside that tire, it exploded! I will never forget that explosion. The tire and I went into orbit. When the dust and I finally settled back to earth, I had three broken bones and multiple bruises and required more stitches—another ambulance ride.

About a month after I finally got my last cast off, I woke up one morning so sick I could not get out of bed. Off to the hospital I went again. This time it was major surgery and several months before I would fully recover. You would think I would have learned and that would be enough, but there was yet one more experience that was mine to have. I then suffered what seemed at the time the worst pain of all—a broken heart.

Finally, weak and too exhausted to be stubborn anymore, I was ready to wave a white flag. I remember the day when I finally bowed my head in prayer and said, "Heavenly Father, Thy will be done." For the first time in my life, I meant it.

The entire direction of my life changed that day. And now, many years later, I don't regret a moment of that painful year; the only thing I regret is that I waited so long to give in. I am convinced that the more total our surrender to Him, the sweeter He will make our joy.

SHAINA'S ROCK

On a recent family camping trip, one of my daughters learned a painful lesson. We came one afternoon to a beautiful camping spot along the Snake River. No sooner had we pulled in than my youngest daughter and one of her older sisters took off exploring. I could just see a four-year-old girl, a ten-year-old girl, and all those cliffs and monstrous boulders. I may be a doting father, but I was a little concerned. So, I warned them.

"Now promise me you won't climb around on these slippery rocks."

"Okay—yeah, sure, Dad—whatever you say." I looked at the older girl and said, "Please make sure that Shaina stays off those rocks. Okay?

"I will, Dad."

I knew I couldn't follow them around forever, so I left them and went back to camp. It wasn't too long before my son came running up to me and said in something of a frantic tone, "Dad, Shaina's hurt."

I bailed out of my camp chair and ran to find her. I met her mother carrying her back to camp cradled in her arms. Even from a distance I could tell that she was hurt. She wasn't just crying; she was screaming. I ran and gathered her in my arms. When I looked down at her face, I was nearly sick. Beginning at the bridge of her nose and spreading outward was horrible swelling and discoloration, and the injury had just barely happened. I asked them what had happened and was told that when her older sister hadn't been with her, Shaina had climbed up on a rock, slipped, fallen, and struck her nose on that same rock.

Her mother and I worked over her for a long time until we were finally able to get her to calm down so we could determine the extent of the injury. As I held her in my arms and she writhed and screamed in pain, I wanted to scream too. I don't know how to say this, but I felt her pain. I would have done anything at that point to have transferred that injury and pain to myself, or at least to have lessened it for her, and I would have done it gladly.

Near the end of the ordeal when she was finally able to find her voice, she whimpered, "Daddy, I wish I'd never crawled up on that rock."

All I could say was, "I wish you hadn't either, Honey."

I've thought about that since it happened. I wonder if that's what it's like for our Father in Heaven. I know that repeatedly He warns us to stay off the rocks, but some of us don't. And if it brings joy to Him when we repent as the Savior said it did, then so too it must tear at His heart when His children suffer. How could it be otherwise?

If you're one of those like me who has slipped on the rocks, or even been pushed off by someone else, I invite you not to suffer alone, but to return to that Father who was called by John *Love*, and to curl up in the arms of His mercy. Let Him cradle you. Cry unto Him in your hour of pain, and I promise that if you do, that your suffering will last only as long and be only as painful as is necessary for your eternal education. Then it will end. He will see to that!

From an experience at Massacre Rocks State Park.

ANGIE'S SOLO

The new year is typically the time of new beginnings. I think they're called "New Year's resolutions." Why do we need the start of a new year as an excuse to change, especially when by the second week of January, our resolve so often tends to fade, which adds to the melancholy of an already cold and blue winter season?

I have a friend who grew up in a musical family. They did a lot of singing publicly and privately, but though she sang with her family, Angie had never sung a solo. From the time she was a child, she had always dreamed of doing so, but like so many of us, fear held her back.

Then, in her senior year of high school, she was approached and asked to sing a solo for a Church fireside. Feeling inferior and afraid, she was reluctant to accept.

But then the thought entered her head, *Why not? I've got to start somewhere; what have I got to lose?*

She agreed and began to prepare. The night of her solo came, and it would be an understatement to say she was nervous.

Then a friend approached her and said, "Angie, this is not a performance, but a teaching opportunity. You are only an instrument in the Lord's hands. If you let the Spirit take over, the message will be carried to the hearts of those listening."

The power of the Lord's Spirit came over her, calming her fears, magnifying her native abilities, and filling her with confidence. I was there. I heard her sing, and it was beautiful; it was powerful, and it was touching.

Since that time, Angie has not stopped singing, and she has been in demand for solo performances. She has been an instrument in the Lord's hands in touching the lives of thousands with His Spirit.

It is with Angie as it is with us: There is a song of many sorts within us all that only needs the power of the Lord's love and Spirit to set it free. If you want to be happier, may your first and foremost resolution be to obey the Lord, and thereby receive the power of His Spirit, which will then set the song within you free.

MOSES AND THE SERPENT

You know, if men were art, some of them would be masterpieces. And I don't think anyone would argue with me if I said that Moses was one them. He was one of the greatest prophets who ever lived. And I would like to share an experience that I believe in part explains why.

When God called Moses to lead Israel out of Egypt, Moses's initial reaction to the call was, "Who, me?"

In response to that, the Lord assured Moses He would be with him, but Moses was still self-doubting and reluctant. Who can blame him?

Finally, the Lord decided it was better to demonstrate to Moses than to explain.

He asked, "What is that in thine hand?" (Exodus 4:2).

Moses answered, "A rod" (Exodus 4:2).

The Lord then commanded Moses to "Cast it on the ground," which he did. And the rod "became a serpent" (Exodus 4:3).

Now, this is the part of the story I really like: "and Moses fled from before it" (Exodus 4:3). Moses was afraid of snakes.

The Lord then said to Moses—and I believe this moment changed all of history—"Put forth thine hand, and take it by the tail" (Exodus 4:4).

What would you do in such a situation? Would you pick up a poisonous serpent by the tail? I get squeamish at simple spiders.

To his everlasting credit, the record says that Moses "put forth his hand, and caught it, and it became a rod in his hand" (Exodus 4:4).

Through this and other experiences, Moses became the great lawgiver who is revered even today. But he was just an ordinary man until the day God called on him to face what he feared and trust in a higher power. That is faith!

What does it mean? Even now, when I don't know why or how or I'm scared to death to try, I know that to obey when the Lord commands is to be fashioned by Him into a "masterpiece."

Adapted from Exodus 4:1–5.

Chopsticks and Jell-O

Not too long ago, I came home from work and immediately sensed that something unusual was going on at the house. As the preparations were being made for the evening meal, I noticed that some of our finer plates and glasses were on the table, and my wife and daughters were looking at me and pointing at me and speaking in hushed tones. I'm a little dense, but that looked suspicious.

When we were called to the table, I noticed a fine-looking meal of Chow Mein—so far, nothing too out of the ordinary. That is until my wife announced we were going to eat this meal with chopsticks—no spoons or forks allowed. Chopsticks. From around the table there came mixed reactions. Some said, "All right!" and others were saying, "Oh no!" I won't tell you which one I was.

The first few minutes of supper were spent giving chopstick lessons. And since none of us was overly chopstick literate, it was a little like the blind leading the blind. However, it didn't take too long before we began catching on. A growling stomach is a powerful motivator. And I'm happy to report it only took me about twice the normal length of time to eat my portion.

One daughter, though, finally gave up and began to cry, "I just can't do it!"

The ultimate test of skill came when my wife produced from the fridge a Jell-O that had not completely set up.

Picture this: There we were, seven hungry people trying every conceivable way to pick up runny Jell-O with chopsticks.

My son finally gave up on the chopstick transfer system and just stuck his face on his plate. Me? I waited until everyone was distracted. Then I grabbed my spoon, and using my chopsticks as a plow, I filled my spoon with Jell-O. In three quick bites it was gone.

I can't remember now whether I got full or just so disgusted I gave up. I do remember, though, that when I was done eating, my thumb and index finger were stiff and sore from working with the chopsticks. But hey, it was worth it! It was a great family memory.

Now the point: Sometimes in life, we are tempted to throw out the old, conventional ways of doing things and try something new. And in many instances, that's a good thing to do because it pulls us out of our ruts and brings zest and adventure to life. But when it comes to moral standards and the commandments of God, none of us has lived long enough or grown smart enough to throw out the combined wisdom of the centuries and the omniscience of God. In other words, finding lasting happiness while breaking the commandments of God is as difficult as eating runny watermelon Jell-O with chopsticks.

To quote a friend of mine, "Folks, it just ain't gonna happen!"

SMILE AT THE STOPLIGHT

Not long ago, I learned a lesson about judging other people and the powerful effect of a smile.

It had been a long day. I'd been up since 2:30 a.m., and I was just rolling to a stop next to a line of cars at the light. I chanced to look at the car next to me and looked right into the innocent face of a beautiful little girl about three or four years of age. To my surprise, she smiled at me—a gorgeous, wide, toothy smile. It was so irresistible that I smiled back. And then, to my total amazement, she blew me a kiss!

I didn't know this little girl, nor did I know her mother, who was driving the car. And there I was driving an old, beat-up, mustard-yellow pickup that had long ago seen better days. My clothes were filthy, my hair was a mop, I had on dark sunglasses, and I sat with one arm propped out the window and a sour expression on my face—and she blew me a kiss?

I was so startled I looked away. As the light changed and the cars began to move, I chanced one more peek at my new friend, and sure enough there she was, still looking right at me. And in a kind of a shy, little-girl way, she was still smiling the same beautiful smile. Oh, she melted my heart.

I drove away from that stoplight with a different attitude. She changed my day entirely. She warmed my heart and cheered my soul.

If I could only keep that day in my memory and follow that little girl's example, I would refrain from judging people by how they appear. Instead, I would love them for what they are—and, like her, I would warmly let them know it.

Little girl, wherever you are, whoever you are, thanks again for brightening my day and being my teacher.

TELEPHONE WIRE

Not long ago while doing some remodel work, I accidentally cut my telephone wire. It had to be repaired. But the area was too small for me to access. I couldn't fit. So, I asked my twelve-year-old daughter if she wanted to learn to wire a telephone. She gave me that look like, "Right, Dad!" but dubiously agreed to help me. I showed her what to do, gave her detailed instructions, and up the ladder she went.

I turned my attention to hanging a door. A few minutes later, though, she was back, standing at my side.

"Oh, man, Dad. That's hard!"

She complained for a few minutes. I encouraged her, and she went back up the ladder. But it wasn't long before she was back again. "Oh, this hurts," she said, working the soreness out of her shoulders and showing me where a staple had scratched her arm.

I smiled, I sympathized, and I sent her back up the ladder, explaining that if she couldn't fix it, I would have to cut a big hole in the wall to repair the damage I'd done.

Over the next thirty minutes or so, she must have come down that ladder four or five more times, each time more frustrated and in more pain. Finally, with only a little bit left to go, she broke one of the wires that she had already spliced, leaving a little, tiny stub so short she could barely get hold of it. That was it—she'd had it! And I knew at that moment, all I had to do was to say, "Oh, don't worry about it, Dear, I'll fix it," and she would have walked away, never again to get any closer to a telephone than picking up a receiver.

But I didn't want to tell her to walk away. I mean, much of my childhood involved failure. For a good part of my life, I believed I was a loser—that I couldn't do anything right. Call me a sap if you will, but as a father, it was important to me that she not fail. I didn't know what to say. So, I told her that she should just walk away for a while, go cool off, and come back later. She took me up on that. She went upstairs, pulled on her sweats, and did something I had never seen her do before: She went running! She was frustrated.

She came back about an hour later. With a renewed sense of determination, she scrambled up that ladder, wedged herself in the ceiling, and about fifteen minutes later she was once again standing at my side.

"All done," she announced. In that short time, she had accomplished twice as much as before. She was grinning so wide you could have tied it behind her ears.

But now came the real test: Was the phone going to work? She picked up the receiver of the once-dead phone. It worked—perfectly!

As we cleaned up, we talked about the experience, and I asked her what she had learned. Among other things, she said something that pleased me so much: "Never give up."

We turned to go upstairs. I asked her, "So how do you feel about wiring telephones?"

She looked up at me with a big smile and said, "Anybody need a phone wired?"

All Creatures of the Spring

I enjoy spring very much. It's my favorite time of the year. It seems to me that as the world wakes up from a long winter sleep and springs back to life, it just sort of takes my soul with it. I really like this time of year.

On one of those first warm days of the season, I couldn't stay inside; I wanted to go outside. So, for a few minutes I took a group of my students, and we went out on the front step of the building. On a whim, I asked them to gather in close and sing acapella the hymn, "All Creatures of Our God and King."

Oh, they could sing! As they did so, a beautiful spirit descended upon the little group. They sang in praise and rejoicing of the masterful hand of the Master Creator. It was powerful; it affected me. As they sang, two squirrels nearby began to chase each other, romping and playing. One of them ran practically under our feet without fear. It was almost like they understood us and were celebrating with us.

At the song's conclusion, the members of my little choir were subdued and reverent. I asked them to close their eyes and turn to face the rising sun. They did so, and we all felt the warmth of it on our cheeks. It felt so good! I then asked them to turn to the north and feel the gentle caress of a slight breeze. They did. I then asked them to be still and listen to the birds that were singing in the nearby trees. They did.

I don't know how to describe it, but we felt something—something wonderful, something heavenly. I declared to them that if they ever want to see the hand of God, they have only to look carefully at His creations. All the earth bears witness in powerful and unmistakable ways of the hand of its Creator, especially at this time of year

I know there's a God, because I have climbed and stood on the high mountains; I've watched the sun rise and set; I've seen the lightning flash and heard the thunder roll; I've sat in a meadow and studied wildflowers. I want you to know that He's there, and this earth is His gift!

THE SWITCH

One day, I was in a hurry to get somewhere when I was stopped by a train crossing the road. You've probably had this happen to you. Slowly that thing rolled to a stop directly across my path. A man jumped off and walked a few yards ahead to a switch. He grabbed the lever, and he moved this tiny section of rail just a few inches, enabling the train to move to a different track and change directions.

Think about that for a minute. Because of these insignificant things called switches, huge trains weighing thousands of tons and being more than a mile long are able to radically change directions and end up at completely different destinations.

So it is with people. The tiniest of influences and decisions can cause the most radical of changes in people's lives, leading them to totally different destinations and different courses. May I share a personal experience along that line?

Many years ago, I was asked to give a church lesson to my friends and college roommates. I suppose that may seem harmless enough, except that it had been only a matter of weeks that I had even begun to consider the existence of God, let alone teach someone else about Him.

I was eighteen years old. I knew nothing about God; I wasn't even sure I believed in Him. Never in my life to that point had I taught any kind of a lesson nor given any manner of a public speech. I didn't have the slightest idea what to say or to do. Needless to say, I was scared to death!

Someone thrust a teaching manual in my hands and said, "Here, just follow this!"

Oh, yeah—as if it were that easy. But that's what I did.

All my friends and roommates gathered in my apartment on Monday night to hear pitiful little me expound "the mysteries of the kingdom." I began as the manual instructed. Then I got to a place where I was told to ask my "audience" a question. I asked the question, but no one answered. They just sat there looking at the floor. I waited, and I waited.

Finally, I blurted out in frustration, "C'mon, you guys, answer me!"

They looked shocked, but they answered me; they came to life, all of them! In a matter of minutes, a marvelous gospel discussion ensued. Looking back, I think that I just smiled and nodded; I had no clue what they were talking about.

Now here's the point: When the lesson was over, a number of them came up to me and complimented me on the wonderful lesson "I" had taught. It might seem like a silly thing, but that had a profound impact on me. It was the first time in my life I could remember feeling like I was actually good at something. I believed what they told me.

Because of that experience, I always and ever after that accepted teaching opportunities that came my way. Eventually I became a professional teacher and speaker.

Again, the influence of the tiniest compliment switched the entire course and destination of my life. I will always be grateful to those wonderful friends.

"George, Do You Know Me?"

On April 12, 1847, in Elm Grove, Iowa, Sarah De Armon Pea Rich recorded in her autobiography, "While here the boy that was with us—George Patten was taken very sick with the Mountain Fever."

George Patten was just a boy. His mother had passed away in Nauvoo, and his father had given him to Charles and Sarah Rich with the request to take him to the Rocky Mountains.

Sarah continued, "And on the 22nd of April 1847, some of the company started on . . . and the boy that was with us—still very sick."

The company traveled on until they reached Garden Grove, Iowa. On May 22, 1847, Sarah wrote, "our boy, George Patten, still got worse and became as helpless as a babe—was out of his head, and to all appearance could not live. Our beds had to be made down in the tent and were fixed comfortable. For the sick boy, all our family did all they could for him. . . . He had by this time become unconscious. Mr. Rich came to my bed and called to me and wanted to know if I could watch over the boy awhile, for he must have a little rest. So, I got up and went to the bedside of the sick boy. . . . [It was] thought the boy could not possibly live many hours. So, I took my seat beside the poor sick boy and began to reason with myself. My reasoning was something like this. I thought to myself this poor dying boy was put into our charge to watch over the same as one of our own children; could we give up one of our own children to die without using all the faith within our reach to plead with the Lord to spare the dear one and not take it away from us; this boy had no mother living to plead with the Lord to spare the dear one. . . . What to do for poor

George—for he was a good boy, and we all loved him. So when I got up from praying I was led by my feelings to put a teaspoonful of consecrated oil in his mouth; his tongue was drawn far back in his mouth and was very black, and his breathing rattling and heavy, and his eyes to all appearance set in his head. I did not see that he swallowed the oil, so I anointed his face and head with the oil, asking the Lord to bless the same; then, in a little while gave him another teaspoonful of oil, asking the Lord at the same time with a humble heart to spare the boy and accept of my feeble efforts in his behalf. I felt broken-hearted before the Lord, and to my great joy, I noticed that George opened his eyes and looked upon me as though he was astonished. I said, 'George do you know me?' He spoke in a whisper, 'Yes.' Oh, how glad I felt by this time. Mr. Rich had woken up and inquired how the boy was, saying afterwards that he almost feared he was gone. I said to him, come and see; the boy looked at him and smiled which astonished Mr. Rich so much that he turned to me and said, 'What has caused such a change?' I said to him, prayer and faith and hope in our Father in Heaven. I told my husband what I had done and how humble I felt while praying to the Lord to spare the boy's life. My husband was truly affected and told me the boy's life would be spared to yet be a blessing to me in some future time. And from that time on the dear boy continued to mend slowly and got well."

In later years, the promise of Apostle Charles C. Rich came to pass. George Patten grew to be a man; settled in Payson, Utah; married; raised a family; and prospered.

Sarah wrote, "Many has been the time that [George] would bring me loads of provisions—butter and groceries when Mr. Rich would be off on missions to forward to the work of the Lord. And when George would help me, he would always say 'Mam,' for that is what he calls me, he would say, 'Mam, I owe my life to you, for your faith and prayers saved me from death.'"

Source: Autobiography of Sarah De Armon Pea Rich, https://www.familysearch.org/tree/person/memories/KWJR-JBT

LORD, I BELIEVE

I have come to the conclusion that parenting is hard! Children don't come with instruction books, but they sure do come with some of the most perplexing problems imaginable. Therefore, I believe that to conscientiously raise a child to maturity is to unknowingly and inevitably raise oneself closer to divinity. Let me illustrate.

While the Savior is on the Mount of Transfiguration with Peter, James, and John, His other Apostles are in the valley below waiting for Him. A man whose son is possessed by an evil spirit comes seeking the Master. Since the Master is not present, the disciples attempt to cast out the foul spirit. But because of their lack of faith, they fail.

When Jesus arrives on the scene, He asks that the son be brought to Him. As the son is brought to the Savior, the evil spirit in the young man throws the son to the ground, where he wallows and foams and thrashes.

The Master asks the father how long he's been like this. The father replies, in other words, "since he was a child. And many times, the evil spirit has tried to destroy him." Then, pitifully, the father pleads, "but if thou canst do any thing, have compassion on us, and help us" (Mark 9:22).

Did this man have faith? Yes—enough to come and ask for help. But it's obvious from what he says that he doesn't have enough faith to have complete confidence in the Master's power.

The Savior, discerning the man's heart and need, says, "If thou canst believe, all things are possible to him that believeth" (Mark 9:23).

Immediately the father cries out with desperate tears what I consider to be the prayer of the ages. He says, "Lord, I believe; help thou mine unbelief" (Mark 9:24).

In other words, this father is saying, "Lord, I need thy help. I have no place left to go. I have faith you can help me, but it's not enough to save my son. Please give me more."

I want you to know that I love the Savior. He answered that prayer, healed that son, and restored him whole to his father. I can only imagine that father's rejoicing.

It is no different now. Is there any prayer a loving Father would be more inclined to hear and answer than that of a desperate, pleading parent?

Parents, we don't need to go this alone—not the raising of our children. In this world today, we can't afford to try it on our own. And I want you to know that God has not relinquished His Fatherhood just because He's granted us custodial care. His love for those children and His ability to help them is greater than ours. And I believe that most of the time He's on our side. It has been aptly said, "One cannot raise heaven's child without heaven's help."

Adapted from Matthew 17, Mark 9, and Luke 9.

THE LUNAR ECLIPSE

One day I came home and heard my youngest daughter say something about an eclipse. I hadn't heard much about it, but I hurried outside, and sure enough, there was only a small sliver of bright light left.

I'm not an astronomer, but I understand that the eclipse was caused by the moon passing through the shadow of the earth, thus blocking the light of the sun. The dark red color on the moon was caused by rays of sunlight that were bent by the earth's atmosphere.

I called the family to come outside. They looked up and ooh-ed and aah-ed accordingly. Some of us wrapped ourselves up in a large Levi quilt and kept watching. We didn't want to miss a thing.

Ever so gradually, the light disappeared. The moon, though still visible, became dark. It fascinated me! I'm a simple-minded soul, and it fascinated me how God works in His heavens to teach us. I felt such a sense of reverence that I began to sing a hymn about the glory of God and His creations. My daughters joined in. It was kind of fun.

The neighbors came out to see what was going on. I'm sure they thought we were crazy, standing out there in the cold serenading a lunar eclipse.

On its steady course, the moon continued to climb higher in the sky, until finally the light reappeared. Now this might seem strange, but the light seemed more beautiful and bright after the eclipse than it did before.

My dear friends, all the creations of God bear witness of Him and of His truth.

We are like that moon. We don't generate our own light; we reflect the light that comes from God. And there are times, and it happens to all of us, when through our own foolishness and rebellion, we block out that light of God that is our source of happiness. It's those times when we need to repent, change our course, and get back into the light.

But—and this is my point—there are also those times, eclipses if you will, when our infinitely wise Father and Teacher allows that brilliant light to be withdrawn through no fault of ours, as He did to Jesus in Gethsemane. Often, these are times of painfully intense testing and growth vital for us all. But know this: Like that moon, the sun's light is not totally withdrawn during these times. If we will hold on and stay the appointed course, allowing God to work His wonders, that light will return—and when it does, it will seem so much more brilliant than ever it did before. Hold on.

THE GENTILE WOMAN

Late in the Savior's ministry, hatred against Him has risen to the point where the Jews are trying to kill Him (see John 7:1). Rejected then by His own, He leaves Israel and goes north into Syria among the Gentiles.

Now, tired and seeking seclusion, He enters a city where a woman identifies Him and cries after Him, "Have mercy on me, O Lord, thou Son of David; my daughter is grievously vexed with a devil" (Matthew 15:22).

The Gospel writers point out something interesting about this woman. She is a Canaanite by birth, a Greek by language and custom, and a Syro-Phonecian by nationality. In other words, she is a pure Gentile, not at all of the blood of Israel (see Bruce R. McConkie, *The Mortal Messiah* [Salt Lake City: Deseret Book, 1980], 3:10).

Considering this, then, how does the Master react to her? He ignores her and keeps right on walking. With faith and persistence, she follows and continues to plead for a miracle on behalf of her daughter. After a time, the disciples become somewhat impatient or annoyed with the woman's pleadings. I mean, after all, Jesus has granted miracles to Gentiles in the past. Why not now?

"Send her away," they say to Him, "for she crieth after us" (Matthew 15:23). In other words, "Lord, give her what she wants and get rid of her" (McConkie, 3:10).

But He answers them, "I am not sent but unto the lost sheep of the house of Israel" (Matthew 15:24). His mortal ministry was to be among the covenant children of Abraham, and later, through the Holy Ghost, among the Gentiles.

The woman then comes directly to the Savior and falls before Him, saying, "Lord, help me" (Matthew 15:25).

His answer to her is most intriguing. "It is not meet," He says, "to take the children's bread, and cast it . . . [to] dogs" (Mark 7:27). It may seem harsh that He refers to her as a dog, but when the Savior used the term *dogs*, a better translation would be "little dogs" or "pet dogs" (see James E. Talmage, *Jesus the Christ* [Salt Lake City: Deseret Book, 1915], 329).

It is as though the Savior is saying to this Gentile woman, "I am the bread of life. The Father has sent me to feed the chosen people of Abraham's lineage. Now is their time to feast, but your time will come" (McConkie, 3:10).

The woman immediately catches His meaning, and to her eternal credit she is not offended, but responds, "Yes, Lord: yet the dogs under the table eat of the children's crumbs" (Mark 7:28).

So impressed is the Lord with this woman's faith that He commends her and grants her request. "[B]e it unto thee," He says, "even as thou wilt" (Matthew 15:28).

The woman returns home to find her daughter delivered and lying on her bed.

This story has troubled many people. Seemingly it portrays the Savior as harsh and rude. Yet, before we pronounce such a judgment, especially without reading the full text, it would be well to consider the scriptural verse that just precedes this story. It reads as follows: "[Jesus] arose, and went into the borders of Tyre and Sidon, and entered into . . . [a] house" (Mark 7:24) "and would that no man should come unto him. But"—and carefully note this—"He could not deny them; for he had compassion upon all men" (JST, Mark 7:22–23).

And so He did and still does. Some of you may actually feel as unworthy as a dog in the presence of the Lord. I bear witness of His compassion and of a mercy so abundant and tender that it still cannot be denied, for you and even for the lowest of us who will repent.

THE WIDOW'S MITE

I f you will pardon my somewhat limited vision, it seems to me that when we consider the rest of the population of planet Earth and the populations of the past, we at the present time are a wealthy and indulged people. I think some would even call us spoiled. I think even the poorest among us would be labeled as rich in some areas of the world. With that in mind, would you consider this story from the last week of the Lord's life?

Jesus stood in the richly furnished courts of Herod's Temple and in the midst of heckling opposition denounced the leaders of the nation for their hypocrisy and their selfish wickedness. The temple, which Jesus had previously called "my house," He now disowned as "your house." The Lord's public ministry among the Jews was over.

Moving away from the open court of the temple, Jesus then entered the Court of the Women, where there were thirteen trumpet-shaped chests that comprised the treasury of the temple. There He sat downcast and in deep sorrow, and probably wept. Then, looking up, Jesus saw a poor widow, known as such by her clothing of mourning, come forward and cast two mites into the treasury. Her offering in American coinage would have been less than half a cent.

Immediately discerning the heart of the situation, Jesus called His disciples to Him and pointed out the deed of the woman, declaring, "Verily I say unto you, That this poor widow hath cast more in, than all they which have cast into the treasury: For all they did cast in of their abundance; but she of her want did cast in all that she had, even [all] her living" (Mark 12:43–44).

I believe it is no accident that Jesus drew attention to this simple deed at this critical time, the end of His public ministry. A walking object lesson, this woman taught the selfish wealthy in simplistic ways among individuals and nations that it is not the size of the offering that counts as much as the heart and the sacrifice behind it.

What about us? Is there someone we should visit? Is there a letter we should write or an offering we should make? I guess I'm just simple-minded enough to believe that time has and will yet memorialize those common people who sacrificed in uncommon ways for worthy day-to-day causes. May the Lord so bless us.

Adapted from Mark 12:41–44; Luke 21:1–4.

DAWNI'S DISAPPOINTMENT

Dawni had prepared for this day for two and a half months. It was the school assembly, and it was her first solo performance on the drums.

It had been a struggle for her to get to this point. Initially, her father had been against her playing the drums, but he had finally relented and said okay in the face of her tears and determination. But, before she was allowed to study and play the drums, she had been required to study another instrument.

Patiently, therefore, she learned the flute, waiting until the opportunity came to play the instrument that was her heart's first desire— the drums. And now that day was here. This assembly was even more significant, since it was the first one that her mother had been able to attend. It was Dawni's big moment. The night before, she spent so much time on her clothes and her hair; she was prepared and so eager.

The band director gave the cue and started the piece. But when Dawni struck the snare drum, no sound came out. Someone or something had misadjusted the drum, making it completely useless. There was no way the director could stop the piece now, so it went on without her. While the other percussionists performed and shined, Dawni dropped out of her chair down onto the floor and desperately tried to repair the damaged drum. She worked frantically, but the piece ended before she could get the drum fixed.

Mother watched it all from the stands, knowing that her dear daughter was in trouble but unable to go to her or help her in any way. At the conclusion of the assembly, Dawni walked out of the crowd and directly to her mother, her eyes swimming with hot tears before she even reached her. She had worked so long and so hard, and the moment was irretrievably gone. It hurt—a lot!

Her mother reached out and took her in her arms, speaking soothingly words of comfort. Her older sister, who was also there, left her friends behind and came to Dawni's side, put her arms around her, hugged her, and offered love and encouragement. The two sisters had only a moment to talk with Mom before going back to class. As they turned to go, Dawni's sister put her arm around her again and said, "C'mon, Dawni, let's go. There's nothing you could've done about it. You did the best you could."

And together they went. Even moments later when kids began to make fun of Dawni, her sister jumped in, defended her, and stayed by her until she returned to class.

Dawni's pain and bitter disappointment did not end there, and it is still not gone. Even as she told me this story, she cried. The pain will probably always be there. But one thing's for certain: The pain was made more bearable because of those who shared it with her.

My dear friends, be there! Just be there! And I promise you love will be so much stronger if you are.

THE STORY OF EASTER

Sometime late Friday afternoon nearing 6:00 p.m., the body of the Lord Jesus was laid by His grieving friends in the borrowed tomb of a rich man, Joseph of Arimathea. It would remain there while His spirit labored elsewhere until the predawn hours of Sunday morning, some thirty-six to forty hours.

Matthew then records:

[Then] came Mary Magdalene and the other Mary to see the sepulcher.

"And, behold, there was a great earthquake: for the angel of the Lord descended from heaven, and . . . rolled back the stone from the door, and sat upon it.

"His countenance was like lightning, and his raiment white as snow:

"And for fear of him the keepers did shake, and become as dead men.

"And the angel answered and said unto the women, Fear not ye: for I know that ye seek Jesus, which was crucified.

"He is not here: for He is risen. (Matthew 28:1–6)

Were there ever more momentous words spoken than those? I think not. The Resurrection of the Lord, as the capstone of His Atonement, is the greatest, most miraculous, and most significant event of all history.

And now again, from the Apostle John:

But Mary stood without at the sepulcher weeping: and as she wept, she stooped down, and looked into the sepulcher,

"And seeth two angels in white sitting, the one at the head, and the other at the feet, where the body of Jesus had lain.

"And they say unto her, Woman, why weepest thou? [And]

She saith unto them, Because they have taken away [the body of] my Lord, and I know not where they have laid Him.

"And when she had thus said, she turned herself back, and saw Jesus standing, and knew not that it was Jesus.

"Jesus saith unto her, Woman, why weepest thou? whom seeketh thou? She, supposing him to be the gardener, saith unto him, Sir, if thou have [hast] borne him hence, tell me where thou hast laid Him, and I will take him away.

"[Then] Jesus saith unto her, Mary." Oh, she recognized that voice. "[And] She turned herself, and saith unto him, Rabboni; which is to say, Master.

"[And] Jesus saith unto her," as she obviously came to embrace Him, "Touch me not; for I am not yet ascended to my Father: but go to my brethren, and say unto them, I ascend unto my Father, and [to] your Father; and to my God, and [to] your God. (John 20:11–17)

So significant was the Resurrection to be to the human family that its reality was to be proven to and attested of by literally thousands of people. They would see Him, touch Him, and know of an absolute certainty of the reality of the Resurrection.

That Judean tomb was empty, and because it was, so shall yours be. And as Jesus rose and ascended into the presence of God, so shall you. And as He arose in glory and splendor to eternal reward, so shall the faithful. But if it were not for that empty tomb, man and all his possibilities here and hereafter would be ended in the gloom of misery and death.

TENDERIZING

Growing up as i did on a ranch in southeastern Idaho, home-grown beef was an abundant part of our diet, and I liked it too. But I remember that some of that beef was tougher than boiled owl. I don't know how old I was, but I well remember walking in the house one day and seeing my mother with this spiked steel mallet thing. She had a raw beefsteak sitting on the cutting board, and she was beating that steak with the mallet for all she was worth.

I asked, "Mom, what are you doing?"

She explained that she was tenderizing the meat to make it easier to eat.

All the years I was at home, I remember my petite little mother beating up beefsteaks.

Lately I have observed a similar phenomenon going on around me. I've seen students, colleagues, and friends being beat up mercilessly by the trials and difficulties of life. Pounded and beaten, their heads bow and the tears course freely down their cheeks. They are being tenderized. My heart goes out to them, but now they are prepared for the refining and sanctifying fire of the Spirit of God, if they will open themselves to it and receive it.

I recall that when the Savior felt a great need for sustaining strength and guidance, He often retired to the wilderness and prayed.

For example, you'll recall after His baptism, being filled with the Spirit of God, Jesus went deep into the wilderness, and for forty days remained there among the wild beasts, fasting, praying, and preparing Himself for His glorious ministry.

On another occasion, on the eve of His calling of the Twelve Apostles, He felt the need for His Father's presence. The Master "went out into a mountain to pray, and continued all night in prayer to God" (Luke 6:12).

And finally, who can forget that in the depth of the Master's suffering in Gethsemane, He set the example for us all. In the seclusion and peace of a grove of olive trees, a place He often went to be alone, the weight of the world's sins pressed down upon Him. He prostrated Himself upon the ground, "And being in an agony he prayed more earnestly" (Luke 22:44).

And so should we.

SARAH AND
THE ANGELS

M y friend Sarah is a single mom struggling to raise two children while going to college herself fulltime. Her day usually begins at 5:00 a.m. with scriptures, prayer, and daily exercise. After getting her babes off to school, she then has her own one-hour commute to college.

One week near the semester's end, in the same week that her daughter Abi was having her eighth birthday party, Sarah found herself with one of those weeks—an extra load of homework, research papers, and two tests to study for. And then, as if that wasn't enough already, she was asked to speak in church. And you know what a burden that can sometimes be.

On the day of Abi's birthday, Abi got extremely sick and had to stay home from school. As the week drew on, Abi did not get better. One night in the middle of the night, Abi cried out in distress for her mother. A blessing was needed—but there was no one to give it. So Sarah prayed, and Abi slept the rest of the night soundly.

The next morning, Sarah began to feel sick as well. And you know how it works in such a situation: Mothers simply cannot afford to get sick. Sarah fasted and prayed and pushed on, feeling more and more physically and emotionally drained. By late Saturday night, sore throat and exhaustion notwithstanding, Sarah put the girls to bed and poured herself into writing a talk that she'd been thinking about all week, but it just wouldn't come!

Somewhere around midnight, Sarah went to bed planning to get up at 4:00 a.m. to finish the talk. But during the night, her younger daughter, Isabelle, awoke and came into Sarah's room with a burning fever. Now both of the girls were sick—and so was Sarah.

Isabelle climbed into bed with Sarah and promptly threw up. Sarah got up, cleaned it up, crawled back in bed, and went back to sleep.

When the alarm went off a short time later at 4:00 a.m., Sarah rolled over and was surprised to see Isabelle wide awake and staring right at her, her eyes as bright and blue as a summer sunrise.

"Mom, who were those two guys?" she asked.

"I—I don't know," Sarah muttered, not quite awake.

Sarah got down on her knees, offered her prayers, and then had the distinct thought that she ought to ask Isabelle about those "two guys."

"What did they look like?" Sarah inquired.

"Humans," came the reply.

"What were they doing?"

As matter-of-factly as a three-year-old can declare, Isabelle said, "Fixing your throat."

Jesus once said to His disciples, "Are not two sparrows sold for a farthing? And one of them shall not fall on the ground without your Father. But the very hairs of your head are all numbered. Fear ye not therefore, ye are of more value than many sparrows" (Matthew 10:29–31). I love that verse.

My friends, we are always and perfectly noticed and known by the Father. He loves us and knows us better than we do ourselves. We do not struggle alone!

Oh, and by the way, as for Sarah—well, she went to church not the least bit sick, and out of that "fixed throat" came a powerful discourse on the Spirit of God.

It's true—and He'll do the same for us.

ROAD RAGE

I have found the world's cure for road rage. Not only that, I have found the way to drive in the worst of conditions almost stress-free. To those of you who feel that the Savior's command to "love your enemies" is difficult enough in normal life, but absolutely impossible in heavy traffic, please consider the following story (see Matthew 5:44).

Recently, a friend of mine was traveling down Interstate 15 from Idaho to Provo, Utah. As she drove, she began to ponder what it would be like to love all men as the Savior commanded. Her thoughts were particularly relevant since she was traveling through one of Utah's most infamous construction zones, with its equally infamous traffic—a stretch of highway where road rage takes on a whole new dimension.

Suddenly, the idea came to her that rather than looking at each car that passed her and thinking, *Stupid driver* or some other such unkind thing, she decided she would look at them and say in her mind as they went by, *I love you.*

She looked over at the driver of the next car that passed her and said in her mind, *I love you.*

Please note: She said this in her mind, not aloud. The Utah Highway Patrol would probably have had her in handcuffs within five miles if she had said it aloud.

She kept doing it, and it actually became fun. All the way from Kaysville on the north to Provo on the south, she told every driver that passed her, *I love you.*

The remarkable thing about this experience was that the more she said it, the more she really felt it. The usual tension and grumpiness that comes with heavy traffic in close quarters wasn't there! Instead, she felt the kind of peace and joy that comes to all those who love as the Savior loves.

When my friend finally got to Provo, there wasn't the usual huge sigh of relief as she exited the freeway. She was actually having fun; she didn't want the trip to end. When she walked in to greet her family, the feeling went with her, and it even intensified. At that moment, she loved all men, even Utah drivers, with a pure love. The warmth of that love lingered for days and left her yearning for its return.

Recently, I was asked how we can come to love people. I have pondered that question deeply, and this is my answer: Just do it! Consider what kind of a world we would have if every driver, every parent, and every person stopped listening to his or her fears and started listening instead to their his or her heart.

My dear friends, we love those we serve, we love those we pray for, and we love most when we give rather than take. In other words, love begins in our actions and moves from there to our heart.

CLIFFORD IN SPANISH

I once felt kind of brave, and I took five active, boisterous children to the public library to check out books. They no more than got in the door than they scattered to all parts of the library to get what they wanted. I didn't check out any books. I went along only to prevent general destruction of the library and harassment of the patrons. After each of them checked out the books they wanted and after I had broken up one game of tag and a wrestling match, we went home with our treasures.

Later that evening, one of my daughters approached me and asked me to read a book to her.

"I'll read it to you tonight when we go to bed," I said.

Late that evening after prayers, my daughter climbed into bed and I sat down by her to read a story. I read her first book—no problem. I read her second book—no problem. Then I picked up the third book that she had checked out, and much to my surprise, my daughter had checked out a book about Clifford the dog—in Spanish. I don't speak Spanish; I can barely speak English.

As I sat there staring at the book somewhat bewildered, my daughter said, "C'mon, Dad, read it."

"I can't, Honey."

"Why not?"

"Because it's in Spanish."

Her answer to that was a classic: "So?"

How do you explain to a five-year-old about language barriers? I couldn't; I didn't know how. And besides that, she insisted that I read it. So, I did what any other intelligent father would have done: I looked at the pictures, and in as confidant a voice as I could, I made up my own story.

I thought about that experience even as I sat there by her bed after she'd fallen asleep. What if that book had been the scriptures, and not *Clifford*? What if she had asked me a question about the scriptures, and I didn't know what to answer? What am I going to say?

"I'm sorry, Honey, I don't speak 'scripture.'"

Speaking as a dad, I wonder how I can help lead my children to their Heavenly Father and His Son if I have to make up my own stories when I look at the scriptures . . . especially when there aren't any pictures?

"Go to the Place of Gathering"

In September 1830, twenty-year-old Chapman Duncan left his home in Barnet, New Hampshire, bound for South America. He was suffering from what was called consumption and decided to go south for his health. The route he chose was to travel to Cincinnati, Ohio, and from there south down the river systems to New Orleans.

While journeying on the Ohio Canal, he became so ill that he was confined to his bed. Somewhere near Louisville, Kentucky, he was lying awake in his bed when he recorded the following experience.

> It appeared as though a man spoke yet I heard no audible voice; it was a quite peaceable yet sure impression in fact I knew that the Lord or an angel spoke to me. This is the message he bore to me:
> "Thou shalt prosecute thy journey no farther south than the mouth of the Ohio river. If you do, you shall die." I looked to see the personage. I saw none. I began to meditate upon what I had heard and the feeling that pervaded my person, and while thinking I cannot say whether it was five minutes or more, the spirit again spake and said further, "If thou wilt go to the place of gathering of my people thou shalt live." The force of the message rested so heavily upon me that I dare not go farther south and turned my course for St. Louis, Missouri.

Chapman became discouraged when he could see no way he could get to St. Louis. He called on the Lord in prayer. Shortly after, he saw two men standing on the wharf. He felt impressed to go talk to them. One of the men was Elder Philo Dibble, a member of The

Church of Jesus Christ of Latter-day Saints. Chapman later recalled, "my soul was filled with joy to think the Lord would make plain the way for me to do his commandments and place means within my reach as he did there."

Chapman set out for Independence, Missouri, in November 1830, driving a wagon for Philo Dibble. He speaks of the warm welcome he received when he arrived.

> After listening to the doctrine of Christ and getting some-what acquainted with the new-made friends (for they took me in), I joined the Church I think the last of December, baptized by Elder Titus Billings on the Sabbath day, con-firmed by Bishop Partridge and council. In a short time the Holy Ghost fell upon me and I did speak with new tongues and prophesy, and I thanked the name of my Redeemer.

And from that point forward, Chapman Duncan cast his lots with the Saints. He lived to be eighty-eight years old and passed away in Caineville, Wayne County, Utah.

Source:www.boap.org/LDS/Early-Saints/CDuncan.html

Max and Joyce

October 11, 1997, dawned a typical Saturday morning for Joyce. As she went for an early-morning walk, her thoughts were of how happy she was and how blessed. She thought of Max, her beloved husband, how much they had grown together, and how the last few years had been the happiest of her life.

As the day progressed, Joyce became involved in the normal Saturday jobs. Max was across the state attending an education conference and would be back late that afternoon. She was excited to have him home.

However, around 3:45 that afternoon, the doorbell rang. When Joyce came to the door, she was met by four close friends and a city police officer. The most awful feeling came over her. She asked them to tell her what she already knew. They explained that Max had been killed in an accident that afternoon.

Joyce said, "My worst nightmare was real. At first, I didn't think I had heard right. How could that be? Things like this didn't happen to me, but to someone else. I remember crying," she said, "until no more tears would come."

Calls went out and family and friends gathered. Finally, sometime after 1:00 a.m., after they had finally made contact with all the family, Joyce went to bed, but not to sleep. She tossed, turned, cried, and wondered if she would just wake up and this would all be an awful dream.

Then, sometime just before dawn, a very special thing happened. Max came to her. She didn't see him; she didn't have to. He was there; she sensed his presence.

Max had never been a very good singer, but he did have three favorite songs, one of which was the great anthem of the pioneers,

"Come, Come Ye Saints." A feeling of love and peace came over Joyce as she heard or felt Max sing, "Why should we mourn or think our lot is hard? Tis not so. All is right."

And so it was. Somehow she was given to know that he was happy and that it hadn't been his choice to leave. But she also knew that he didn't want to come back.

Since that sad day, the saddest of her life, Joyce has never felt closer to her Savior, and Max's presence has been with members of the family several times administering much needed comfort.

In closing, I'd like to share why I tell this very personal story. Not long ago as my family was gathered one evening, we got into a discussion about the Second Coming of Christ. My older children were peppering me with questions about it, and they were difficult questions. Suddenly, my six-year-old daughter, Hannah, who was sitting on my lap and who I suppose was just a little bored with the present topic, reached up, grabbed my head, and pulled it down where she could speak in my ear.

"Daddy," she said, "when you die, will you be my guardian angel?"

It took a minute for me to answer. As I did so, a wonderful feeling came over me.

"Honey," I said, "there's no place I'd rather be."

Personal experience of Max and Joyce Wilson of Blackfoot, Idaho; used with permission.

Bad Things to Good People

I n my occupation, I often hear questions like these: "Why do bad things have to happen to good people?" "Why is life so unfair?" And the hardest of all these questions: "If God really loved us, how could He let this happen?"

Well, I don't know all the answers, but maybe this story will lend some comfort.

Late one evening, years ago, my youngest daughter was toddling around in the kitchen. She was at that awkward stage where she was walking, but not all too steadily. I was upstairs getting ready for bed, and my wife was somewhere in the house. All the children were in bed except for Shaina.

Suddenly I heard a thump and a terrible cry. I ran downstairs and found Shaina lying on the kitchen floor screaming. Evidently, she had crawled up on a chair and fallen off face first onto the floor. When I scooped her up, her face was covered with blood. I ran for the bathroom, and quickly realized we were going to have to take her to the hospital.

When we got there, the doctor examined the wound and told us that if it was not stitched back together, it would leave a horrible, ugly scar. I remember that we put our tiny daughter on the table, but when the doctor began to operate on her, her whimpering cries turned into panicked screams once more. We had no choice. We had to strap her to the table and place her head in restraints. Still, that was not enough. She screamed and thrashed wildly. Finally, the doctor told me that I was going to have to sit down and hold her head still.

I sat down near her head and put a hand on each side of her head; I forcefully held it still while the doctor gently and expertly stitched her lip back together. I will never forget her screams and her cries, but most of all, I will never forget those accusing eyes that stared up at me and seemed to say, "Daddy, how could you do this to me? Let me go!" It tore my heart to do that to her, but I did not let go.

The doctor finished, and the wound healed with only a minor scar.

Shaina has been terrified of doctors and hospitals ever since. I'm not even sure she's forgiven me for that night. From her perspective, all she could see was her father inflicting horrible pain and torment on her. But from my perspective, the pain was only a temporary thing and was very much worth the end result. Shaina may not see it now, but she'll see it later when she matures and her perspective changes. I daresay, given the same circumstances, she would even do the same for her children.

Once when the Lord's people were suffering greatly from the trials and inequities of life, He said to them, "Be still and know that I am God" (D&C 101:16). And when the children of Israel were trapped against the sea, and it looked as though God had led them into the wilderness to die, Moses stood before them and declared, "Fear ye not, stand still and see the salvation of the Lord" (Exodus 14:12).

Remember what the Lord said through Isaiah: "My thoughts are not your thoughts, neither are your ways my ways" (Isaiah 55:8).

My dear and wonderful friends, especially those of you who are suffering, in spite of how much it may hurt now and make absolutely no sense, I promise you there will come a day if we are faithful when we will see, understand, and agree.

LIVING ON THE EDGE

One night my daughter Sherise and I were walking side by side on the boardwalk through Norris Geyser Basin in Yellowstone. All around us were the boiling pots so characteristic of the park. We'd read the signs going in telling us that those boardwalks were there for our own safety, and that we'd better stay on them.

As we strolled along, Sherise suddenly stepped out on the very edge of the boardwalk and began a sort of balanced walking still holding my hand. I jerked her back into the middle of the boardwalk.

"But, Dad," she protested, "I want to walk on the edge."

I couldn't resist. Seeing an opportunity to teach, I said, "Do you know what that means?"

The look she gave me told me that she had no clue what I was talking about. I explained to her that "walking on the edge" is what some people call "living on the edge." It means they're always flirting with danger. They push the limits of safety, seeing just how far they can go and just how much they can get away with.

All the while I was explaining this, Sherise was still out there dancing on the edge. I could see that she'd heard me, but the message hadn't registered. So while she skipped merrily along, I sidled over—and with a quick jerk of my hip, I bumped her off the boardwalk near one of the hotpots.

"Dad!" she protested indignantly.

She scrambled back up before she got caught walking where the law said she shouldn't. She gave me one of those looks that's hotter than the water she'd been standing by.

When she was back up beside me, this time in the middle of the boardwalk, I said, "Now, why shouldn't we walk on the edge?"

"'Cause we might fall off," she said.

"Now do you understand?" I asked.

She nodded her head, and for the rest of the trip I never again caught her walking on the edge. And I hope I never do for the rest of her life.

Whether we're speaking of our physical safety or our spiritual health, it is the same. Walking or living on the edge is dumb and dangerous. It wouldn't be so bad if Satan weren't walking right by us, but he is. He's just waiting for us to get out on the edge.

Don't be fooled. Satan's not a guy in a red suit with little horns and an attitude. He's real! His hatred is real, and his vigilant opposition is constant. If we live on the edge, sooner or later, he will push us off into forbidden territory. And I assure you, the pain and the effort it takes to get back once we're off is just not worth the risk or the thrill.

And one last thing: For those who find themselves already off the boardwalk and trying to get back on, thank God we have a Savior with an outstretched hand.

EMMELINE

President David O. McKay said that "man's extremity is God's opportunity."

One brisk October morning, Emmeline, her sister MaryAnn, and her younger brother Nathan were in the family van on their way to school. As they rounded a corner, Emmeline was momentarily blinded by the rising sun. She had scarcely begun to press on the brakes when the sun suddenly vanished behind a truck.

At nearly fifty miles per hour, the van slammed into the back of a slow-moving semi. The horrendous force of the impact drove the dashboard into the front seats, breaking both of MaryAnn's legs. The restraining lap belt seriously injured Nathan in the back seat.

As Emmeline regained consciousness and realized what had happened, her first thoughts were of her brother and sister and that she had killed them. Panic ripped through her. Crying and screaming, she struggled to free herself, but the steering wheel and dash had her hopelessly pinned. Then suddenly, Emmeline realized that she was not alone as a voice spoke clearly and distinctly in her ear.

"Emmeline, it's okay. You're the one that is hurt the worst. Your brother and sister are fine."

Emmeline screamed, "It really hurts; I want out!"

"Emmeline, you have to have patience. This is going to take a long time, but when you compare this to eternity, it will be only a couple of minutes. Be patient."

Emmeline stopped struggling and screaming as a feeling of divine peace and well-being filled her soul. So radically did her demeanor change that rescuers standing nearby panicked; they thought she had died!

Paramedics and rescue crews continued to work quickly to cut MaryAnn and finally Emmeline free of the wrecked vehicle. All the while they worked, Emmeline, in spite of horribly painful injuries, was calm, basking in a divine presence. That presence attended her and comforted her until the time that she was taken into surgery some seven hours later.

I am reminded of a particularly powerful passage of scripture:

> The Lord is my Shepherd; I shall not want. He maketh me to lie down in green pastures: he leadeth me beside the still waters. He restoreth my soul: he leadeth me in the paths of righteousness for his name's sake. Yea, though I walk through the valley of the shadow of death, I will fear no evil: for thou art with me; thy rod and thy staff they comfort me. Thou preparest a table before me in the presence of mine enemies: thou anointest my head with oil; my cup runneth over. Surely goodness and mercy shall follow me all the days of my life: and I will dwell in the house of the Lord for ever. (Psalms 23)

HANNAH HENDEE

Wisdom picks her battles in matters of principle and fights them fiercely. May I illustrate?

On October 16, 1780, a band of three hundred Indians under the command of a British captain named Horton moved down the White River near South Royalton, Vermont, capturing, killing, and terrorizing the local inhabitants. The Hendee family was warned of the oncoming mobbers. The father set out to warn others of the danger while Mrs. Hendee fled into the woods with her children, seven-year-old Michael and a younger daughter.

As they ran, they came headlong into a band of the mobbers. An Indian stepped from behind a tree, grabbed her son, and wrestled him away. She demanded to know what they were going to do with him.

One of them who spoke English replied, "Make a soldier of him."

They dragged the sobbing boy away. Mrs. Hendee made her way toward the road carrying her tiny daughter, who was screaming in panicked terror.

As she traveled down the road, surely as heartsick and grief-stricken as any mother could be, she was suddenly filled with a surge of steeled resolve and a fierce determination. They could not, they would not keep her little boy!

She went back and faced Captain Horton. Oblivious to the looming danger, she demanded of him her little boy. Horton responded that he could not control the Indians, and it was not his concern what they did anyway.

Angry and indignant, Hannah Hendee said, "You are their commander, and they must and will obey you. The curse will fall upon you for whatever crime they commit, and all the innocent blood they shall shed will be found in your skirts when the secrets of men's hearts shall be made known, and it will cry for vengeance upon your head!"

Her son was brought in. Hannah grabbed his hand and refused to let go. One of the men standing nearby grabbed her son and jerked him away from her, threatening her with a cutlass. Defiantly, she faced the man and grabbed the boy again, telling them that she would follow them every step of the way to Canada if she had to. She would never give up; they would not have her son.

This was a unique and singular confrontation: A lone, determined mother fighting for that which she loved and cherished against a mob of bloodthirsty, unprincipled men.

How does the story end? Later that day, the British soldiers and the Indians set out on their march with their captives. Hannah Hendee left that camp and crossed the river for home. But when she did, it was with her daughter, Michael, and eight other little boys she had rescued from a sure and certain death.

Has this kind of will to fight died in America today? No, I think not. Is there a need to be roused to fight today? There is! For what should we be roused to fight? Please hear my answer: Our God, our religion, our freedom, our peace, our wives, our children, and our families. Lord help us that we may be roused to fight!

Adapted from Evelyn Wood Lovejoy, History of Royalton, Vermont (Burlington, Vermont: Free Press Printing Company, 1911), cited in The Spirit of America (Salt Lake City: Bookcraft, 1998), 43–46.

COURTNEY'S SECOND CHANCE

An experience of a young friend of mine serves to teach a powerful principle. Courtney loves music. She plays the piano and the flute; she sings; she composes; she can do it all. She's wonderfully talented. In a state high school solo competition, she won top honors her sophomore and junior year playing the flute, and for a high school musician, the state solos are the pinnacles of achievement. To win is to be the best in the state in a highly competitive discipline.

Now it's Courtney's senior year. She has prepared longer and harder than ever before for her solo. Winning the state solo competition again would be a dream come true. Confident, but a little nervous, she faces the judge in the preliminaries. If she does well here, she goes to state. The judge gives the signal, and Courtney begins to play.

But all of a sudden, she makes a little mistake—then another one—then another one! At that point the judge lowers her head and begins writing. This makes Courtney even more nervous, and she makes more mistakes, until finally her concentration is completely gone, and it's all she can do to keep from breaking down and crying. She finishes the piece and walks out holding back the tears and knowing in her heart that her chances of going to state are gone—permanently!

She knew she wouldn't go to state and that she wouldn't get a second chance.

Courtney walked home very slowly that day reliving, over and over, as we so often do, those terrible mistakes that had cost her so dearly.

"Oh, how I longed for a chance to prove myself," she said, "to show the judge I really could do it, that I really was worthy of going to state." But there was no way—not now. Her little mistakes in a weak moment had irretrievably cost her the opportunity of a life-time.

That night, as Courtney continued to ponder on the day's events, a thought suddenly struck her. With the judge there was no second chance, but with God there always is.

"If we make a mistake in this life," she said, "our chance to return to our Father in Heaven is not lost. We have 'a second chance.' We have a chance to prove ourselves to the judge of heaven that we can pass the test. It we make a mistake, we have the opportunity to make it so that it doesn't count against us. It will be forgotten."

As these thoughts passed through her mind, the Spirit of the Lord passed through her soul. Peace and power overshadowed the pain of the day's disappointment. That night as she went to bed, it wasn't the agonizing memory of failure that filled Courtney's mind—it was a deeper love and a more profound gratitude for the Lord Jesus Christ, the eternal God of "the second chance."

Based on the experience of Courtney Gardner, Spring 2000.

ENOS

P arents, this story is for you. One day, I was helping my children get off to school, and I noticed they weren't listening to me. Several times I reminded them of various family rules, only to have to turn around and remind them again just a few minutes later. Is there some sort of teenage disorder called *parentally induced selective deafness* that makes them unable to hear me? I know I wasn't like that as a kid.

If this sounds at all familiar to you, I would like to share a story that gives me hope that maybe—just maybe—I'm not wasting my breath.

There was a young man who grew up in a good home. His parents were faithful people who made a conscientious effort to see to the proper teaching and training of their children. This young man heard what his parents said; he listened. But as is so typical of youth, he heard with his ears but not with his heart. He didn't fully understand the importance of what he heard, and like so many youth, he made mistakes in his life that left him with that acute pain of guilt.

One day, while he was out on a hunting trip, his mind, probably sparked by the beautiful surroundings he was in, turned from the hunting of animals to the hunting of something else: peace and self-respect. It was as though he looked at himself in the mirror, soul and all, and didn't like what he saw. Guilt and self-loathing swept over him. There had to be more to life than this. And at that point, a powerful sense of yearning, a hungering many times more painful than a missed breakfast, gnawed at his soul.

And then, it came into his mind what his father had so often taught him about the happiness and the peace that comes to the faithful both in this world and in the world to come. And suddenly, more than anything else in the world, he wanted that happiness. He wanted to know for himself what his dad had taught. He wanted to change, to be a better person, to be forgiven of his sins and have this terrible burden of guilt lifted from him. And I love this: What he did next is what he had seen his parents do hundreds of times. He dropped to his knees and he began to pray—not that routine kind of prayer so common at bedtimes and mealtimes. No, it was real prayer; it was mighty prayer, that kind so filled with reaching and sincerity that its power lifts the heart and mind of the one who prays from this fallen world to a perfect one. His whole soul was reaching to God.

And the voice of the Lord came into his mind and spoke peace to his soul. His sins were forgiven, and by the miracle of Christ his guilt was swept away. And once more, the cycle of the ages was complete where the child discovers for himself the wisdom, the power, and the rightness of his parents' oft-repeated words.

This young man's name was Enos. Enos became a prophet and gave the rest of his life to the service of God, thanks to his parents.

Now parents, I plead with you: With all the love and power of your heart, teach truth, over and over again if that is what it takes, and someday when that hungering moment comes for your children, they will know where to turn for nourishment and what to do.

Adapted from the book of Enos.

THE FLAGPOLE

I was taught in Church once that we sometimes make the gospel too complicated. It really is plain and simple. So in the spirit of heavenly simplicity, may I share a simple story?

My son was searching for an Eagle project to complete the requirements for his Eagle Scout Award. After some searching and connecting with the right people, he decided to build and install a flagpole at a friend's place of employment.

He worked hard, as did others, putting in the required forty hours just in the preliminary work of obtaining the materials and preparing them for installation. Some very generous and kind people helped him. Then, just days before he was to install the flagpole, he received a phone call telling him that the project was off. His friend had received instructions that no flagpole was to be put in for any reason.

Jed had a real problem. The materials were bought, and he had substantial donations of time, money, and effort, most of which was unreturnable. What was he going to do? He had a flagpole and nowhere to put it.

Well, he went to work harder. For two and a half months, both of us looked for somewhere else to install the pole. We explored every option we could think of, all to no avail; nothing panned out. Finally, on a Saturday in mid-March, our last option fell through.

That night as Jed went to bed, he knelt to pray, and he asked the Lord to help him with his Eagle project. Later that same night as I went to bed, I also asked the Lord for help.

The next morning at church, I was helping in the nursery with the children; so was Scott, one of Jed's Scout leaders. Cheryl, a friend, walked in. She struck up a conversation with Scott about various things, and then suddenly out of nowhere she said, "Scott, I need someone to do an Eagle Scout project. I need someone to put in a flagpole for me where I work."

Scott looked at her like, *You have got to be putting me on.* But when he realized she was serious, he jumped on it immediately, made the appropriate connections, and my son was off and running once more.

You can call that what you will, but the whole thing is very interesting to me. That was the first time Cheryl had ever been in the nursery, she had no previous knowledge of Jed's predicament, and that very same week she sold her home and moved from the area.

Some may say it was just a coincidence, and that's fine if they do. But as for me, I believe in Heavenly Father. I believe He hears and answers the prayers of fifteen-year-old Scouts whose backs are against the wall. I believe He hears the concerns of parents who want their children to succeed. And most of all, I believe He loves us.

My dear friends, isn't there sufficient reason in your life right now that you and He could have a serious conversation?

Mama's Boys

Long ago in a faraway, ancient land, a terrible war raged between two mighty armies. An innumerable army of evil invaders had taken many cities. The defenders struggled day and night on many fronts to maintain the cities they had and to reclaim those they had lost, but they were too few and spread too thin. However, heaven justified their cause because they were unlike the invaders who fought for power, land, and conquest. The defenders fought in defense of their families, their freedom, their rights, their liberty, and their religion.

Treachery and treason among the ranks of the defenders, though, had cost them dearly and had weakened their strength when they needed it most. They were now in desperate circumstances, so desperate it seemed that they might lose all, when from out of obscurity came a small band of youth—teenagers, boys if you will—numbering some two thousand. They armed themselves with weapons of war, a covenant to fight to the death, and mighty faith in God. So armed and much needed, they set out and joined forces with their brothers on the southern front.

A plan was devised in which the boys would pass near the fortifications of the strongest army of the enemy to decoy them out. According to the plan, the boys passed the city of the enemy, and the bloodthirsty invaders poured forth against them, sensing an easy victory. The boys began to run, pretending to be scared, which caused the enemy to pursue with great vigor. It also allowed the balance of the defenders to fall in behind the duped invaders between them and their stronghold.

The plan was for the main army of defenders to catch the invaders from behind, outside of their fortifications, and defeat them in open-field battle. But it went awry; the invaders perceived the trap and sped their march after the boys and away from the main army. If the boys turned back, they'd be turning back to certain death. So they marched on, staying just out of reach of the enemy.

On the third day, the pursuing invaders suddenly stopped, leaving the small band of boys uncertain whether they were being lured into a trap or if their fellow defenders had caught their pursuers from behind. They didn't know.

With faith in their God that they would be delivered from whatever might happen, they turned back, only to discover that the two great armies were locked indeed in mortal struggle. But alas, it was their friends who were giving way, not the enemy. With fury and power born of faith in the living God, they threw themselves at the enemy, causing the entire army of the invaders to turn on the small, heroic band of boys. But they stood firm! Their fellow defenders rallied, and the army of the invaders, frightened by the ferocity of a group of boys, was surrounded and compelled to surrender. The victory was won. The strongest army of the invaders in that part of the land was defeated.

The great miracle of this ancient battle was that *not one* of those boys fell among the thousands of dead and wounded on both sides. All stood! All lived! And all would fight again! In large measure, that band of boys was responsible for saving the freedom of their country.

And what of those boys? Where did they learn such faith, such undaunted firmness against evil? In their own words, they said, "We do not doubt our mothers knew it" (Alma 56:48).

And so is the power of a mother, and never was it needed more than now.

RUTH

In an age when it seems to be more and more fashionable to be fickle, faithless, and an infidel, there is a story in the Old Testament that is inspiring and refreshing.

During a time of famine in ancient Israel, a man named Elimelech moved his family from Bethlehem to the country of Moab. While there, Elimelech died, leaving behind his wife, Naomi, and two sons. The two sons married Moabite women. It wasn't long before the two sons also died, leaving Naomi alone. Naomi heard that the famine had ended in Israel, and she set her mind to go home. Orpah and Ruth, her two daughters-in-law, went with her.

Somewhere near the border between the two countries, Naomi begged the two girls to go back, to return to their families and make themselves a new life; she had nothing to offer them. After many tears, Orpah kissed Naomi and went back, disappearing into history. Ruth, on the other hand, would not turn back.

"Entreat me not," she said, "to leave thee, or to return from following after thee: for whither thou goest, I will go; and where thou lodgest, I will lodge: thy people shall be my people, and thy God my God: Where thou diest, will I die, and there will I be buried: The Lord do so to me, and more also, if ought but death part thee and me" (Ruth 1:16–17).

Powerful words, but they were not empty drama. In making such a declaration, Ruth would be leaving behind the family of her childhood to follow an impoverished old woman from whom she stood to gain nothing. Ruth would leave behind the country, the customs, and the traditions she had grown up with to enter a strange new land and society that did not always look with favor upon foreigners. And perhaps most significant of all, she would be denouncing the religion and the God of her upbringing for the strange new worship of Jehovah.

Ruth was a virtuous woman filled with faith and loyalty. She stayed with Naomi, and, true to her word, labored to support her and never left her. Then and now, Ruth's loyalty was noticed and honored.

I've thought about this and that quality we call *loyalty*. Loyalty is a quality stronger than iron in the human soul that binds us to causes, promises, country, spouse, and family. It holds us firmly in that place where we committed ourselves to be, especially when there's no other reason to stay other than "we ought to." History will always honor those loyal to the last measure for true causes. And in that spirit, Ruth was no exception. For her undying loyalty and devotion, Ruth would find much joy in Israel. By an intriguing chain of events, she would marry a righteous Israelite named Boaz, and to them would be born a son named Obed. Obed had a son named Jesse. Jesse had a son named David.

Ruth was to be honored for all time as the great-grandmother of David, Israel's mightiest king.

And that's not all. Matthew makes a special mention of Ruth as being an ancestress of the greatest man who ever lived, the Lord Jesus Christ.

Stick tight where you ought to be. Be loyal, whether it be to your cause, your country, your spouse, or your children. Don't let the opposition pull you out of place.

Adapted from Ruth 1.

"God Helps Those Who Help Themselves"

In 1855 near Dundee, Scotland, Betsey's mother announced to her daughters that they were going to America with the handcart companies the next season. The oldest son was already there and working a farm near Lehi, Utah. Betsey says the girls laughed but the spirit of the gathering filled them, and they went to work. Soon they were able to pay their passage for Zion. In May 1856, they bid farewell to their "dear old Scotland."

In her late years, now as a widow, Betsey Smith Goodwin was asked to write her memories of the trail. These are some of her most profound recollections.

> On the 15th day of July, 1856, we rolled out of the Iowa City camp, on our way to cross the plains with handcarts. Our captain was James Gray Willie, and his counselors were: Millen Atwood and Levi Savage. There were 120 handcarts and six wagons, and about five hundred people, sixty-six of whom died on the journey.
>
> I will not dwell upon the hardships we endured, nor the hunger and cold, but I like to tell of the goodness of God unto us. One day, especially, stands out from among the remainder. The wind blew fresh, as if its breezes came from the sea. It kept blowing harder until it became fierce. Clouds arose, the thunder and lightning were appalling. Even the ox teams ahead refused to face the storm. Our captain, who always rode a mule, dismounted

and stepped into the middle of the road, bared his head to the storm, and every man, as he came up, stood by him with bared head—one hundred carts, their pullers and pushers, looking to their captain for counsel. The captain said, "Let us pray." And there was offered such a prayer! He told the Lord our circumstances, he talked to God, as one man talks to another, and as if the Lord was very near. I felt that he was; and many others felt the same. Then the storm parted to the right and to the left! We hurried on to camp, got our tents pitched, and some fires built, when the storm burst in all its fury!"

Another circumstance I remember clearly. My mother was taken very sick with cramp and cholera. A very fatal trouble in our weakened condition. We all felt bad about mother. I remember thinking, "Many are dying: mother may die, and what a dark world it would be without our dear mother!" As I gathered the sage to burn on our camp-fire, I couldn't keep from crying. When I met mother, she asked me what was the matter. I told her how badly I felt.

She said, "Do not feel like that; pray for me. I have been out yonder in the snow praying to the Lord to spare our lives, that we might get through to the Valley. I will never murmur nor complain, whatever we pass through, when we get there. God heard our prayers, and she kept her word. Even when, in years following, she went blind with age, she never murmured."

About three miles on this side of Green River, as I was walking ahead of the train, leading my little brother of six, and encouraging him along by telling him stories of what he would get when we arrived at the Valley, he said: "When we get to that creek, I wish we could see our brother Rob."

I said, "Come along, maybe we will, when we get to the top of the bank."

When we arrived at the top of the bank and looked down we saw a wagon with just one yoke of oxen on. We had never seen the like before, so we waited on the summit until they should pass. The man stared at us, and as his team came beside us, he yelled, whoa, to the oxen. It was then we knew him. He jumped off the wagon and caught his sisters in his arms as they came up with the cart. How we all wept with joy! The cart was then tied behind the wagon. Little Alex climbed into the wagon as happy as a prince, instead of a poor, tired child.

The next question from Rob was, "Where is mother and Sister Mary?"

"They are behind somewhere, Robby. You will find them by the road." Mother was still sick, and when she stopped to rest she had to lie down; she could not sit up. Some had died that way; they would go to sleep and never awaken. Mary was afraid that mother would do likewise, and tried to arouse her by telling her about a team coming with only one yoke of cattle on.

Mother replied, "Well, never mind, Mary; don't bother me; I am so tired."

"Well, mother, the man is running this way. It surely is Robert."

"O, no, Mary; that would be too good to be true!"

Well, she was soon convinced, as Robert took her in his arms and helped her into the wagon. As he did so, mother exclaimed, "I couldn't be more thankful to get into the kingdom of heaven than I am to see you and lie here and rest."

Explanations followed. Robert stated that he had suffered from a mountain fever and was just recovering when he received a letter that we were coming. He then borrowed and hired an outfit to come and meet us. None too soon!

And then Betsey concludes with this testimony:

"And now Brother Editor of the *Era,* you said you would like my story. I have therefore written these few recollections. For the benefit of the youth of Zion who may read this, I bear testimony that God hears and answers prayers, and the Lord will help those who help themselves"

And so He does!

Betsey Smith Goodwin, aged seventy-three, Beaver Utah.

TURN TO PRAY

I was recently taught something in the scriptures that deeply affected me.

Where did the Savior go immediately after His baptism and just before the ministry that would end with His life?

He went out into the wilderness to fast and to pray for forty days in close communion with His Father. Why?

And again, where was the Master on the eve of that crucial day when His most trusted friends and associates who would be with Him in His ministry—namely the Twelve Apostles—were to be chosen and ordained?

The Savior was on a Galilean mountain where He spent the better part of the night in prayer with His Father.

And yet again, where did the Savior with a troubled heart turn when the multitudes misunderstood Him and tried to make Him king against His will?

He went to the mountains. And again, He spent the better part of the night in prayer with His Father.

When the missionaries He had sent out came back, rejoicing in their great success and the miracles they'd seen, what was the Master's reaction?

I'll quote: "In that hour Jesus rejoiced in spirit, and said, I thank thee, O Father, Lord of heaven and earth, that thou hast hid these things from the wise and prudent and hast revealed them unto babes" (Luke 10:21). And He rejoiced in prayer with them.

And lastly, in those monumental moments of Gethsemane, when the fate of all humanity hung in the balance and Jesus was in the deepest agony of any mortal ever known, where did He turn for strength?

He turned where He had always turned—to His Father.

"Abba, Father, all things are possible unto thee; take away this cup from me: nevertheless, [not my will but thine be done]" (Mark 14:36).

"And being in an agony," Luke records, "he prayed more earnestly: and His sweat was as it were great drops of blood falling down to the ground" (Luke 22:44).

Do you see the point I'm trying to make?

As part of my weekly church assignment, I was tending the little children in the nursery. Ah, I love to be there. Down on my hands and knees, I was having a wonderful time with them when the door suddenly opened. I turned and looked, and there stood tiny little Luke, not yet two years old, with his Daddy not a step behind him.

I called to him, "Hi, Luke!"

He took one look at that strange, ugly creature on the floor, and he spun about and buried his face in his father's knees, clinging to him desperately for protection.

Ah! Luke reacted instinctively to what he considered a threat. He turned to the surest security he knew—his father.

Where do we turn? Where do we turn when we're happy? Where do we turn when we're sad? Where do we turn when we need strength or counsel? Don't turn to the world. I pray that our relationship with our Heavenly Father will be so close, so constant, and so personal that it is our deepest nature and first impulse to turn to Him, and only Him, in all our moments of need.

PEACE

Twenty years ago, I seldom even heard the word *stress*. Now, it seems I hear it every day from young and old alike. Are we a stressed-out generation? Is the pace of our lives destroying the peace of our lives? This story is intended to be a gentle reminder to us all.

One night, at the Savior's command, the Apostles went in a ship with Him to cross the Sea of Galilee. Being weary, Jesus went to the stern of the boat and was soon asleep on a pillow.

An unusually violent storm arose, blowing down from the surrounding mountains. Huge waves broke over the boat, filling it with water until it was on the verge of sinking.

The disciples were terrified. Coming to the Master, they awoke Him saying, "Master, carest thou not that we perish?"

The Savior arose immediately and rebuked the wind, saying unto the sea, "Peace, be still!" Instantly, the wind abated and there followed a great calm. The disciples were astonished at Him. They knew He had power, but because their fear had overruled their faith, they failed to comprehend how far-reaching His power actually was.

If He can calm as angry sea, surely He can calm a troubled heart. He is the one and only source of lasting peace. So much so is He the giver of this great gift that Isaiah calls Him the "Prince of Peace"—a prince to whom I would hope we will be subjects at any sacrifice.

CHANGE

I am convinced that almost anyone can change. The purpose of life is to change. The sacrifice of the Savior insured that. And to me no character in the scriptures exemplifies change more than the Apostle Peter.

Three times on the night of the Savior's betrayal, Peter denied Him, and that after publicly proclaiming that he would never forsake the Savior. The record says that after the third denial, the cock crowed, and Peter went out and wept bitterly.

I can only imagine the depth of Peter's pain and guilt at what he had done. Surely it must have been one of the lowest points of his life. I've often wondered what thoughts filled his mind during those three days that Jesus was in the tomb. Could it have been something like, "There's no hope for me now; I can never be forgiven. My sin is too great; I've sinned too much. How could He ever love me again?'

Well, if the story of Peter's life had ended there, it would have been a tragedy indeed. But it didn't. On the day of the Resurrection, Peter was privileged with a personal visit from the Risen Lord, face to face, one on one. Peter was forgiven and once more encircled in the arms of the Savior's love. It changed Peter. That change is dramatically illustrated by an event that occurred some two months later.

Late one afternoon, Peter and John walked into the temple. As they passed through the gate called "Beautiful," a man crippled from birth begged alms of them.

"Look on us," Peter commanded (Acts 3:4).

The man looked at them, expecting to receive something of them, but Peter said, "Silver and gold have I none; but such as I have give I [unto] thee. In the name of Jesus Christ of Nazareth rise up and walk" (Acts 3:6).

Peter reached down and lifted the man to stand on feet that had never borne weight. "[W]alking, [and] leaping, and praising God," the healed man entered the temple rejoicing (Acts 3:8).

Under the refining hand of the Master, Peter's denial became the catalyst for his change. Eventually he became like the Master he worshiped, a man of miracles, eventually even a martyr.

I believe that Peter is a pattern for all those who want to change. Whether we are now in the rock bottom of bitter tears and regret for past mistakes, or simply stranded on a plateau of complacency, when invited the Savior comes and will encircle us in the arms of His love. And the effect? We are changed; we are never again the same.

Acts 3; Gordon B. Hinckley, Ensign, *May 1979.*

PEACE ON EARTH

The night the Savior was born, angels sang in the heavens, "Glory to God in the highest, and on earth peace, good will toward men" (Luke 2:14).

Peace! Think about that. Of all the words the angels could have said to tell us what the birth of a Savior would mean, they said *peace*! The Lord Jesus is peace! Christmas is peace! I'd like to share a story from another land and a long time ago.

The nation was torn apart. Contention and hate filled the land. On one hand, there were those, few in number, who believed in the eminent coming of Jesus Christ to this earth. On the other hand, there were those, by far the majority, who refused to believe in the words of the prophets and who would not accept the coming of Christ. Every sign and miracle that was manifest was explained away by the unbelievers either as a coincidence or a lucky guess. Religion came to be seen in the land as a wicked and seditious tradition. The persecution that began as simple, annoyed gossip soon grew into deadly threats and violence.

Suddenly, there arose a group of the non-believers who declared that the time was past for the Messiah to be born. Their words raged throughout the land like a forest fire, causing a tremendous uproar. People caught hold of them and joined in. While the people of God held firm in the faith, the wicked plotted their death. A date was set apart and plans were made to execute the people of God for their belief in the coming of Christ.

Finally, it came to climax. The next day, those who had believed in the ancient traditions of the coming of Christ were to be murdered by their own countrymen. While the wicked prepared to murder, the righteous prayed mightily all that day.

Then, miracle of miracles: That night as the sun went down below the horizon, it didn't get dark. To the utter astonishment of all the people, the land remained as light as though it was midday. A new and glorious star arose in the heavens. The people recognized it as the long-promised sign of the birth of Christ.

While the faithful rejoiced in their deliverance, the unbelievers fell to the earth in utter astonishment. Fear and the spirit of repentance came upon them.

The next morning as the sun arose, the light of faith arose with it. And this is interesting: All thoughts of murder and contention were swept away by the spirit that filled the hearts of the people. Peace and good will reigned throughout the land.

That day on the other side of the world, He who would be called the Prince of Peace was born of Mary and laid in a manger. It intrigues me that even in His birth, He who would someday be Savior of us all saved His people even as a tiny babe.

Of all things, Christmas is peace! Christ is peace! Now as then, all who will let the daystar arise in their hearts will know for themselves of a surety the blessing invoked by the angels that first night: "Peace on Earth, good will toward men."

Adapted from Helaman 16 and 3 Nephi 1.

THE LOCKSMITH

Not long ago some friends and I traveled to another city where I was to speak. I remember that as we carried our stuff inside to set up, I broke with my usual pattern of putting my keys in my suit pocket, and I dropped them in my book bag instead.

The meeting was fun, and the people were wonderful. When it was over, I picked up my book bag and all of our stuff and I carried it out and put it in the van. I noticed as I did so that I also put in the van a purse belonging to one of the group. As I did so, I thought, *I'd better not leave that thing in the van unlocked.* So I stepped back, I hit the power locks, and I shut the door.

No sooner was that door shut than I grabbed for my pockets. Yeah, my keys were locked in the van. I tried all the doors and windows. That van might as well have been Fort Knox. With my tools and skills, there was no way I was going to get into that van without breaking a window. I felt kind of foolish. I went back and admitted what I had done. The others just laughed and took it all in stride.

But we had a predicament. We are miles from home and locked out of our vehicle late in the evening. Worse, I don't personally know anyone in that town who could help me. There happened to be a couple of good-hearted fellows there who took pity on us, and they began making phone calls. After making a bunch of calls, they managed to reach a fellow who owned a body and fender shop. I was impressed. He dropped what he was doing and immediately came over.

As we sat there and watched, he took out his toolbox, and in less time than it takes me to tell this story, he had that door open. He made it look so easy, because for him it *was* easy.

When it was all over with and we were inside the van, I offered to pay him. He refused. He could have made me feel like an idiot or that

I had greatly inconvenienced him, but he didn't, nor did the others who were there who helped me. A number of them stood by, chatting with us until we loaded up and drove off. I tell you I left that town with the neatest feeling toward those wonderful people, especially a kind man skilled with locks.

You might wonder what this has to do with anything. My dear friends, there is a lesson herein. Who among us has not locked ourselves out of the kingdom or out of heaven by our own foolishness? No matter what we did, or said, or tried, there was no way for us to get in. We simply didn't know how. Then along came caring friends, family, or Church leaders who called on the master locksmith on our behalf. And He came, and with kindness and with gentleness unlocked the door of heaven for us. Without the Lord Jesus Christ, we would literally be out in the cold eternally.

I have a conviction: Christ is mighty to save; He is very good at what He does. To those of you who struggle with discouragement and disappointment because you just can't be as good as you want to be, and you feel that there's just no hope, I have a word of advice. Step aside and let the Master work.

FORWARD
MOMENTUM

When I was just a boy, my dad and I went deer hunting one Saturday. In order to get to where we were going to go to hunt, we had to travel over a small mountain pass in central Idaho. As we approached the pass, the road became slick with fresh-fallen snow. I didn't pay much attention to the snow until we came to a steep, banked curve on the pass. The curve turned left and banked away from the mountain to a steep drop-off. As we went into the curve, the car slid sideways with the back end threatening to slide off the mountain. I remember I was convinced at the time that we were going to die. I panicked and yelled for Dad to stop. Strangely, he just grinned—you know that kind of grin that says, "I know something you don't"—and he said, "I can't stop."

I thought he was crazy. If we didn't stop, we were going to slide off the mountain backend first and roll forever. Quickly he explained that as long as he kept the rear wheels going forward, we were less likely to slide off. I still don't think I believed him—that is, until just a moment later when something forced him to stop. And as soon as he did, in spite of the fact that the brakes were locked up, we began to slide backward, out of control, toward the edge. Now I really panicked! I remember looking out the back window of the car, and all I could see was sky.

Coolly, my dad threw the power again to the rear wheels, and they began to dig and scratch and spin. We stopped sliding. It seemed like it took forever, but gradually we inched our way around that curve, the car straightened up, and we went on our way.

I will be forever grateful to a father who understood a simple principle: unless there is power applied in the forward direction, we will slide backward, not stand still.

So it is with life. The road to our heavenly home is slick, steep, and fraught with many perils, and there is no standing still. Either we are going forward or we are sliding back. The power must be continually applied. How?

Well, each time you and I keep the commandments, pray, and search the scriptures, individually or with our families, we throw the power to the wheels once more and move forward. And I know that sometimes it seems like you're only moving inches if you're moving at all, and you wonder if it's worth the battle and the opposition. But I promise you that if you persist in these righteous things, just as my Dad saved me, by the grace of God you'll save yourself and your family.

GETHSEMANE

After all the stories we've told, there yet remains one story more important than any other—the Savior's Atonement in the Garden of Gethsemane. This is a story that needs to be heard and understood by anyone who has ever wrestled with the bitterness of guilt and the blush of shame, by anyone who has ever felt burdened and inadequate, by anyone who has ever felt worthless and alone, and by anyone who has ever felt that life had no purpose and was not worth living.

After the singing of a hymn, Jesus and the Twelve Apostles leave the upper room where they partook of the Last Supper and make their way out of Jerusalem to the Mount of Olives. Taking Peter, James, and John, Jesus enters the Garden of Gethsemane, a place where olives are grown and then crushed under intense pressure to extract their life-sustaining oil.

Jesus invites the three Apostles to "tarry . . . and watch" (Mark 14:34).

He then goes about a stone's throw away and collapses face-first to the ground, praying, "O my Father, if it be possible, let this cup pass from me: nevertheless not as I will, but as thou wilt" (Matthew 26:39).

After some time in prayer, Jesus returns to the three Apostles and finds them asleep. Jesus wakes them, saying, "What, could ye not watch with me one hour? Watch and pray that ye enter not into temptation" (Matthew 26:40–41).

Jesus leaves them again, and again in incomprehensible physical and spiritual agony brought on by the sins of all mankind and the onslaught of all hell itself, He bows beneath the load and prays,

"O my Father, if this cup may not pass away from me, except I drink it, thy will be done" (Matthew 26:42).

Luke records that "there appeared unto Him an angel from heaven, strengthening him. And being in an agony he prayed more earnestly: and his sweat was as it were great drops of blood falling down to the ground" (Luke 22:43–44).

When He returns the third time, the Apostles are again asleep. Shortly, Judas comes and betrays the Master with a kiss. Jesus is then arrested, and with a rope around His neck, He is led away eventually to the cross where His atoning sacrifice is completed.

The Savior took upon Him in that garden the sins, pains, sicknesses, and infirmities of His people. His Atonement was an infinite burden of sin. For that moment in time, He who knew no sin and guilt became for us the greatest sinner of them all.

Truly, He is our compassionate high priest that can "be touched with the feeling of our infirmities" (Hebrews 4:15).

He understands us and can help us as no one else can.

By virtue of His precious blood shed from every pore of His body, He stands between us and justice, pleading our cause eternally.

The Atonement of Jesus Christ is not a legend of long ago and far away. It is a vital truth, an active principle so intimate and intertwined with our daily existence that even now we would fall in profound gratitude if we had even a mustard seed of a glimpse.

I tell this sacred story because more than anything, I want the hopeless and overwhelmed to have hope. I know how much He can help. Therefore, "Let us . . . come boldly unto the throne of grace, that we may obtain mercy, and find grace to help in time of need" (Hebrews 4:16).

"He Did Strengthen Them"

During a recent study of the Book of Mormon, I saw something that I have never noticed before. I was reading Alma 2 in which Mormon tells the story of the rise of Amlici, a cunning activist who wanted to be king and to destroy religious liberty among the Nephites. The question is put to a referendum, and Amlici loses the vote. He rises up in rebellion against the will of the people and gathers an army. It comes to battle. The prophet and chief judge, Alma the Younger, leads his forces into battle against the Amlicites. The forces of Amlici are routed, slaughtered, and scattered.

Amlici and his remaining army meet and join up with a Lamanite invasion force and march toward Zarahemla. Alma is apprised of the alliance and rushes toward Zarahemla to stop the overthrow of the capital. The two armies meet at the Sidon River.

The forces of the Lamanites and Amlicites vastly outnumber the Nephites. They attack the Nephites while they are crossing the river, a very vulnerable and dangerous position for Alma's people to be in. Knowing their weakness, the Nephites "prayed mightily to [the Lord] that He would deliver them out of the hands of their enemies, therefore the Lord did hear their cries, and did strengthen them, and the Lamanites and Amlicites did fall before them" (Alma 2:28–29).

What is unexpected and wonderful is that Alma, the commander-in-chief, is in the midst of the pitched battle. He squares off with Amlici himself, and they begin to fight face to face. Mormon writes, "And it came to pass that Alma, being a man of God, being exercised with much faith, cried, saying: O Lord, have mercy and spare my life, that I may be an instrument in thy hands to save and preserve this people. Now when Alma had said these words, he contended *again* with Amlici and he was strengthened, insomuch that he slew Amlici with the sword" (Alma 2:30–31).

Alma didn't stop there. He then squared swords with the king of the Lamanites, who hastily retreated and sent his guards to fight Alma. I would presume that the best fighters would comprise those who guard the king. Nonetheless, Alma and his guards "slew and drove them back" (Alma 2:33).

Then, notwithstanding the Lamanites "were so numerous that they could not be numbered," they ran, and the Nephites won the day (Alma 2:35).

Alma was in the heat of pitched battle. He prayed to God for strength to beat Amlici. He was physically, mentally, and emotionally strengthened by the Almighty to defeat his opponent. As far as the record shows, Alma was not an experienced fighter. He was not a Captain Moroni, and yet he was out front leading his men into battle. Morever, he was not a young man. It is likely that he was at the high end of fifty to sixty years of age. He was given the physical strength and power of will to fight the day to victory.

Of all the stories he could have shared from that period, why did Mormon choose that story for us? Perhaps to teach us this principle: If we pray in faith for the strength to beat our enemies and win our battles, it will come. To our bodies, minds, and hearts, strength and power will come! And it does not matter what our enemy may be that day—sufficient unto the day will be the strength thereof, if we pray. Even if my enemy that day is me!

Source: Alma 2.

INDEX

A

Abed-nego, refusal to stop praying, 102–103

Adversities
> painful year of, 135–136
> tenderizing effects of, 168–169

Airplane, landing in the dark, 33–34

Alfalfa, sheep gorging on, 22

Allelopathy, 21

Alma, victory over Amlici, 215–216

Altars, often made of rocks, 69

Amlici, rebellion of, 215–216

Answers, to prayer, 119–120

Armies, vision of in the heavens, 65–66

Army
> Alma's, 215–216
> Gideon's, 104–105
> Midianite, 104–105

Atonement, 98
> as explained by little girl, 61–62
> testimony of, 91

B

Babcock, Amos, 130

Band-Aid, used as object lesson, 109–110

Battle
> engaged in by stripling warriors, 194–195
> vision of in the heavens, 65–66

Beef, tenderizing, 168

Bicycle
> hitting curb, 73
> injured in accident on, 135

Birth, signs of Jesus's on American continent, 207–208

Black walnut trees, kill plants around them, 21

Blizzard, on cross-country ski trip, 79–80

Blood, shed by Jesus, 91

Boanerges, nickname given to
James and John, 19
Breaking, a horse, 77–78
Burial, of Jesus in tomb, 98

C

Cancer, pancreatic, of young
husband and father, 28–29
Car accident, Spirit spoke to driver,
184–185
Car door, locked, prayer about,
119–120
Cattle drive, 121
Change, as purpose of life, 205
Child
> drank medicine in kitchen, 41
> running around on stand at
> church, 2–3
Chopsticks, eating with, 143–144
Christmas, story of in Luke, 56–57
Christus, inspiration while viewing,
115–116
Church lesson, teaching first,
151–152
Church talk, offered by woman
healed of sickness, 170–171
Clawson, Cornelia, journey to Mis-
souri, 130–131
Clawson, Ebenezer
> healing of, 130–131
> thrown from wagon, 130
Clawson, Moses
> feelings at baptism, 130
> journey to Missouri,
> 130–131
Clawson, Rudger, description of
woman raised from dead, 84–85
Clifford, girl checked out Spanish
version, 174
Climbing, Tetons, 96-97, 106–108
Commandment, to love one another,
113
Consecrated oil, used to heal
George Patten, 154

Creations, appreciation for God's,
149–150
Cross-country skiing, getting lost
during, 79–80
Crucifixion
> description of, 98
> impact of on little girl, 61–62
Curb, bicycle crashing into, 73

D

Daddy, little girl's name for father,
48
Dark, landing airplane in, 33–34
Dead, woman raised from, 83–85
Deaf man, healed by Jesus, 124
Deafness, parentally induced selec-
tive, 190
Death
> coping with sorrow of, 75–76
> woman predicts her own, 83
Devil
> cast out of young man by
> Jesus, 156
> cast out of young woman by
> Jesus, 160–161
> intent of, 106
Devils
> casting out of man and into
> pigs, 134
> man possessed by, 134
Dibble, Philo, assisting Chapman
Duncan in travels, 176–177
Dirt, object lesson using, 88–89
Discipline, God's style of, 55
Discouragement, of Elijah, 8–9
Door, missionaries laughing at, 1
Driver, young woman in accident
hears Spirit, 184–185
Drum, misadjusted, ruin's girl's
solo, 164–165
Duncan, Chapman, led to place of
gathering, 176–177

E

Eagle, project involving flagpole, 192–193

Easter, story of, 166–167

Eclipse, lunar, comparison to life, 158–159

Edge, walking on near hotpots, 182–183

Eiffel Tower, experience of homesick musician at, 43–44

Eliasson, Anders, paid for immigrants to Zion, 64

Elijah
> healed by the Spirit of God, 8–9
>
> running to the wilderness, 8
>
> witnessing the powers of nature, 8

Elisha, healing Naaman of leprosy, 117–118

Enoch, vision of God weeping, 39–40

Enos, prayer of in response to parents' teaching, 190–191

F

Faith, 29, 86–87
> necessary for miracles, 124

Family, importance of in eternity, 53

Family prayer, Vaughn Featherstone's desire for, 31–32

Fasting, Jesus spent forty days in wilderness, 202

Father
> pleads with Jesus to heal son, 156
>
> prompted to check on child in kitchen, 41

Fear, Moses challenged to face, 141–142

Featherstone, Vaughn, desire for family prayer, 31–32

Fisher, Rufus, 130

Flagpole, needed for Eagle project, 192–193

Flute, solo, mistakes compounded in, 188–189

Focus, maintain through distraction, 73

Forty days, Jesus fasted and prayed in wilderness, 202

Foundation of righteousness, Jesus referred to as, 69

Furnace, three Hebrews thrown into, 102–103

G

Gama globulin shot, child's prayer about, 67–68

Garnet Canyon saddle, climbing, 96

Gathering, place of, Chapman Duncan led to, 176–177

Gentile, woman, seeks healing from Jesus, 160–161

Gethsemane, experience of Jesus in, 213–214

Gideon
> armies of, 104–105
>
> army's defeat of Midianites, 105

God
> style of discipline, 55
>
> weeping in Enoch's vision, 39–40

Goodwin, Betsey Smith, recollection of handcart journey, 198–201

Gould, John, 130

Grand Teton, experience climbing, 96–97

Grandfather, hit in head by toddler, 113–114

Greene, John, vision of armies in the heavens, 65–66

Handcart journey, Betsey's recollection of, 198–201

Happiness, in difficult situations,

28–29

Healing
in the name of Jesus,
126–127
of boy thrown from wagon,
130–131
Heavenly Father, likened to father
of prodigal son, 101
Hendee, Hannah, facing Indians
who kidnapped son, 186-187
Hendricks, Drusilla, 12–13
how she supported family, 12
husband shot by mob, 12
son joined Mormon
Battalion, 12–13
Hendricks, William, joined Mormon
Battalion, 13
Hope, 29
Horse, challenges of breaking,
77–78
Husband, spirit of appearing to wife,
178–170
Hymn, sung by deceased husband to
wife, 178–179
Hymnbook, blood on page of,
90–91

I

Idol, erected by King Nebuchadnez-
zar, 102
Immigrants, given money by Anders
Eliasson, 64
Indians, faced by woman whose son
they kidnapped, 186–187
Injuries
from breaking a horse, 77
overcoming to compete in
Olympic trials, 71–72
Intimacy, lesson about using soil,
88–89
Isaiah 53, 81–82

J

James, given nickname by Jesus, 19
Jell-O, eating with chopsticks,
143–144
Jensen, Ella, raised from the dead,
83–85
Jensen, Hans, 83
Jensen, Jacob, 83
Jesus
acknowledging the weeping
woman, 49
as Advocate, 36
as Friend, 36
as Prince of Peace, 204
asking "whom say ye that I
am?" 37
blood of, 91
burial of in tomb, 98
calming the storm, 204
commanding disciples to
love one another, 113
comparisons to Passover
lambs, 6–7
driving moneychangers from
temple, 92
experience of in Gethse-
mane, 213–214
giving His Apostles nick-
names, 19
healing man on the Sabbath,
111–112
healing through His name,
136–127
healing young man possessed
with devil, 156
healing young woman
possessed with devil,
160–161
identity of, 37–38
mediator for prayerful father,
35–36
mission of to save all, 90
palsied man lowered through
roof to, 14–15
prayers of, 202–203

prophesied destruction of
temple, 92–93
resurrection of, 99–100
rumored to be John the
Baptist, 37
saved Peter from sinking
in water, 86
signs of birth on American
continent, 207–208
Son of God, 38
testified of in Isaiah, 81–82
ultimate offering for sin, 7
walking on water, 86
woman touching His robe,
10–11
John the Baptist, Jesus rumored to
be, 37
John, given nickname by Jesus, 19
Joy, in affliction, 123
Juniper trees, kill plants around
them, 21

K

Kidney stones, 24–26
Kimball, Heber, vision of armies in
the heavens, 65–66
Kimball, Vilate, vision of armies in
the heavens, 65–66
Kiss, young girl at stoplight blowing
a, 145

L

Lambs
Passover, comparisons to
Jesus, 6–7
used as sacrifices, 90
Lame man, healed by Peter, 126
Laughing, missionaries at door, 1
Lava rock, used as object lesson,
69–70
Lee, Harold B., hit on head by
toddler, 113–114
Leprosy, Naaman healed of,

117–118
Lesson, church, teaching first,
151–152
Lewis, C.S., quote about Jesus as
Son of God, 38
Locksmith, kindness of, 209–210
Love
expression of by Jesus to
praying man, 128
feelings of for other drivers,
172–173
given as new commandment,
113
Lower Saddle, climbing, 106
Luke, Christmas story, 56–57
Lunar eclipse, comparison of to life,
158–159

M

Magdalene, Mary, at resurrection of
Jesus, 99–100, 166–167
Malmberg, John Peter
desire to journey to Zion, 63
paid back money for
immigration, 64
Marathon
family at finish line of, 53
running of, 52–53
Mary Magdalene, at resurrection of
Jesus, 99–100, 166–167
Meshach, refusal to stop praying,
102–103
Midianites, battle against Gideon's
army, 104–105
Miracles
depend on faith, 124
possible when you believe,
17–18
song lyrics about, 18
Missionaries, laughing at door, 1
Missionary, returned, holding child
on lap, 2–3
Mistakes
compounded in flute solo,

188–189
overcoming, 5
Mite, widow's, 162–163
Mob, shooting of Drusilla Hendricks's husband, 12
Momentum, forward, of rear wheels prevented accident, 211–212
Moneychangers, driven from temple, 92
Moon, Elder, 130
Mormon Battalion, Drusilla Hendricks's son joined, 12–13
Moses
    casting rod into serpent, 141
    challenged to face fear, 141–142
Mother-up, behavior of cows, 121
Movies, objectionable scenes in, 50–51

N

Naaman, healed of leprosy, 117–118
Name, power of, 126
Naomi, led Ruth to Israel, 196–197
Nebuchadnezzar, King, erected idol, 102
Nicknames, used by Jesus for Apostles, 19
Norris Geyser Basin, experience in, 182–183
North Visitors' Center, refuge from thunderstorm in, 115

O

Object lesson
    using a Band-Aid, 109–110
    using a stomachache, 109–110
    using lava rock, 69–70
    using orange juice, 50–51
    using soil, 88–89
    using sunset, 45

using toilet water in orange juice, 50–51
Obstacles, overcoming, 71–72
Offense, none taken at cabin in the snow, 46–47
Oil, consecrated, used to heal George Patten, 154
Orange juice, as object lesson about movies, 50–51
Orpah, returned from following Naomi, 196–197
Overconfidence, leads to injuries, 78

P

Palsied man, lowered through roof to Jesus, 14–15
Pancreatic cancer, of young husband and father, 28–29
Parentally induced selective deafness, 190
Parents, praying for return of son, 30
Paris, experience of homesick musician in, 43–44
Passover lambs, comparisons to Jesus, 6–7
Patten, George, 153–155
    healing of with consecrated oil, 154
Peace, message of Jesus's birth, 207, 208
Perfection, attaining, 97
Peter
    change of, 205–206
    denying Jesus three times, 205
    healing lame man, 126, 205–206
    so named by Jesus, 19
    validating Jesus's identity, 37
    walking on water, 86
Pigs, casting devils into, 134
Pillars, often made of rocks, 69

Power, of God, 134
Pray
    commandment to, 30–32
    Jesus going to wilderness for
    forty days, 202
Prayer
    about gama globulin shot,
    67–68
    about locked car door,
    119–120
    homesick musician in Paris,
    43–44
    inspired, 95
    of Enos, in response to
    parents' teaching, 190–191
    of father in family argument,
    35–36
    recognizing answers to,
    119–120
    regarding flagpole for Eagle
    project, 192–193
    saves Alma's army, 215–216
    Vaughn Featherstone's desire
    for, 31–32
Prayers
    consider carefully, 95
    of Jesus, 202-203
Prodigal son, parable of, 101

R

Rail, moved a few inches changes
train destination, 151
Rescue, of children from Indian
band, 186–187
Resurrection
    description of, 99–100
    hope for, 75–76
    Mary Magdalene at, 99–100
    testimony of, 100
Returned missionary, holding child
on lap, 2–3
Rich, Charles C., 153, 154
Rich, Sarah De Armon Pea, healing
of George Patten, 153

Road rage, antidote for, 172–173
Rock of Salvation, Jesus referred to
as, 69
Rock
    girl injured on, 137–138
    lava, used as object lesson,
    69–70
Rocks, used to make altars and
pillars, 69
Roof, palsied man lowered through,
14–15
Ruth, faith of to follow Naomi,
196–197

S

Sabbath, Jesus healing man on,
111–112
Sacrifices, as important as victories,
72
Scriptures, importance of reading to
children, 175
Sea of Galilee, storm on, 204
Second chances, always possible
with God, 189
Serpent, Moses casting out of rod,
141
Sexual relations, lesson about using
soil, 88–89
Shadrach, refusal to stop praying,
102–103
Sheep, gorging on alfalfa, 22
Signs of the time, discourse on, 93
Simon, named Peter by Jesus, 19
Simon the Pharisee, Jesus eating at
home of, 49
Sing
    taking students outside to,
    149–150
    young woman frightened to,
    139–140
Skiing, cross-country, getting lost
during, 79–80
Skunk
    efforts to free, 132

sprayed by, 132

Sleigh, pitched out of, 135

Smile, powerful effect of, 145

Snow, Eliza R., in spirit world, 85

Snow, Lorenzo
  patriarchal blessing of, 85
  raised woman from dead, 84–85

Snow, whitewashing of students in, 46–47

Snowfield, obstacle in climbing Tetons, 106–108

Soil, object lesson using, 88–89

Solo
  drum, ruined by misadjusted instrument, 164–165
  young woman frightened to sing, 139–140

Son, prodigal, parable of, 101

Son of God, C.S. Lewis quote about, 38

Song
  lyrics about miracles, 18
  woman taking comfort from as mother died of cancer, 16–18

Sons of thunder, nickname given to James and John, 19

Sorrow, from death, overcoming, 75–76

South Teton, experience summiting, 97

Speech impediment, healed by Jesus, 124

Speeding, state trooper's warning about, 54–55

Spirit world, described by woman who died, 85

State trooper, warning about speeding, 54–55

Stevens, John, 130

Stomachache, used as object lesson, 109–110

Stoplight, young girl smiling at, 145

Storm
  on Sea of Galilee, 204
  on Temple Square, 115
  on Teton mountains, 123–125

Storms, why God allows, 123–124

Stripling warriors, 194–195

Sunrise, reflections on, 109

Sunset
  reflections on, 109
  used as object lesson, 45

Swimmer, overcoming injuries to compete, 71–72

Swine, casting devils into, 134

Switch, used to move train to different destination, 151

T

Teacher
  as a shepherd, 22
  as king of the town, 58

Teachers, pleas to, 58–60

Teaching, a sacred trust, 22

Telephone wire, challenging daughter to fix, 147–148

Temple
  driving moneychangers from, 92
  Jesus prophesied destruction of, 92–93

Tenderizing, effects of adversity, 168–169

Teton mountains, climbing, 96–97, 106–108, 123–125

Thanksgiving, Vaughn Featherstone's desire to pray on, 31–32

Thumb, sliced open in accident, 135

Thumbnail, injured, 90–91

Thunderstorm, on Temple Square, 115

Tire, explosion of, 136

Toddler, hitting grandfather in the head, 113–114

Toilet water, in orange juice, as object lesson, 50–51

Tomb, burial of Jesus in, 98

Tooth fairy, 94–95
Toradol, shut down kidneys, 24–26
Train, moves to new destination by switch, 151

V

Vision, of battle in the heavens, 65–66

W

Wagon, healing of boy thrown from, 130–131
Warriors, stripling, 194–195
Water retention, during treatment for kidney stones, 24–26
Water
       Jesus walking on, 86
       Peter walking on, 86
Water-skiing, mishaps, 4
Weeping, Enoch's vision of God, 39–40
Whitewashing, of students in snow, 46–47
Widow's mite, 162–163
Withered hand, man with healed on Sabbath, 111-112
Woman
       experience of losing husband in accident, 178–179
       Gentile, seeks healing from Jesus, 160–161
       touching Jesus's robe, 10–11
       weeping at Jesus's feet, 49

Y

Year, of adversities, 135–136
Yellowstone, experience in geyser basin at, 182–183